THE STATE THEORY
OF MONEY

BY
GEORG FRIEDRICH KNAPP

ABRIDGED EDITION, TRANSLATED BY
H. M. LUCAS AND J. BONAR

Martino Publishing
Mansfield Centre, CT
2013

Martino Publishing
P.O. Box 373,
Mansfield Centre, CT 06250 USA

ISBN   978-1-61427-496-4

© *2013   Martino Publishing*

Cover design by T. Matarazzo

Printed in the United States of America On 100% Acid-Free Paper

THE STATE THEORY
OF MONEY

GEORG FRIEDRICH KNAPP

ABRIDGED EDITION, TRANSLATED BY
H. M. LUCAS AND J. BONAR

Published on behalf of the Royal Economic Society by
MACMILLAN AND CO., LIMITED
ST. MARTIN'S STREET, LONDON
1924

PRINTED IN GREAT BRITAIN

AUTHOR'S PREFACE TO THE ENGLISH EDITION

The State Theory of Money appeared first in 1905; the 2nd edition followed in 1918, the 3rd in 1921, the 4th in 1923. Our translation is based on the 4th.

When the work had appeared in Germany, it was reviewed in England by Dr. J. Bonar in the *Economic Journal*, March 1922.[1] The somewhat unfamiliar features of the book could not have been more happily brought out than in this review.

Thereupon the Royal Economic Society determined to set on foot an English translation, in an abridged form. The work consists of four chapters, of which only the first three will be found here, translated with masterly exactness in spite of all difficulties. The fourth chapter contains the history of currency in England, France, Germany and Austria, as shown in the Contents. The author would not have advised this omission; but the ground is perhaps one of expense and lies in any case beyond his criticism.

Moreover, the same curtailment was made in

[1] Vol. xxxii. pp. 39–47. Mr. C. P. Sanger had reviewed it as early as June, 1906, in the *Economic Journal*, vol. xvi, pp. 266–267.

the Japanese translation by Kiyozo Miyata, Tokio, 1922;—it might seem as if German writers laid greater stress on history than foreign writers.

In any case the author is grateful to the Society for carrying out the undertaking, doubtless at some sacrifice. In particular my thanks are due to Messrs. Keynes and Bonar, as well as to the honoured translator, Mrs. Lucas, and her adviser, Mr. Sanger.

G. F. KNAPP.

Darmstadt,
May 16th, 1924.

AUTHOR'S PREFACE TO THE FIRST GERMAN EDITION (1905)

I GAINED my earliest impressions as to currency questions in 1861 from a summer journey in the Tirol, where there was only paper money in circulation. I had my first teaching on the subject the following winter in Munich from Staatsrat von Hermann. My teacher was a well-informed and clear-sighted man, a silver metallist and an upholder of the theory that the use of paper money was based on credit. In the winter of 1862–63 his favourite subject was currency conditions in the United States, and I was again among his hearers.

When in Strassburg I myself began a small course of lectures on currency, I tried to keep theory in the background and to bring out clearly what is matter of rule and ordinance [1] in the most important States, and I still think this heuristic method the best for lectures.

One of my pupils, Karl Helfferich, has far outstripped me in this art; for clearness of construction his works cannot be praised too highly. Another pupil, Philipp Kalkmann, by his studies on England, Holland and Switzerland, has greatly increased my knowledge. I would gladly have had him with me as an associate, had he not adopted another profession.

In the autumn of 1895, in a course of lectures in Berlin, I put forward my views fully for the first time, laying down: that the money of a State is not what is of compulsory general acceptance, but what is accepted at the public pay offices; and that the standard is not chosen for any properties of the metals, but for the deliberate purpose of influencing exchanges with the commercially important neighbouring States.

Soon after this Georg Simmel brought out his able book on the *Philosophy of Money* (Leipzig, 1900). As it treats only of the sociological side of currency, I do not need to regard my work as competing with his. I feel myself nearer to Otto Heyn, whose work (1894) is entitled *Paper Standard with a Gold Reserve for Foreign Trade* (Papierwährung mit Goldreserve für den Auslandsverkehr). It was a book that appealed to public men and deserved more attention

[1] *Das Pragmatische.*

than it received. For myself, I came to give up any attempt to influence public men, and I give the first place to the theory or philosophy of the subject, at the risk of displeasing both schools of monometallists, not to speak of the bimetallists, who will not be any better satisfied.

On the other hand, I hope for the approval and perhaps the help of those who take the monetary system (or, better, the whole system of payments) to be a branch of political science. I hold the attempt to deduce it without the idea of a State to be not only out of date, but even absurd, however widely these views may still obtain. To avoid polemics, I have always called this the metallistic view, and have opposed metallism as such without naming its supporters, and also without opposing the use of metal.

I began to develop the State Theory of Money in September 1901, and I dare not confess how many false starts I made. A theory must be pushed to extremes or it is valueless. The practical man can, nay, must, content himself with half-truths. The theorist who stops short at half-truths is lost.

In order to attain my end and replace the metallistic view by one founded on Political Science, I was forced to invent a terminology of my own. Even if new expressions could have been formed in German, it seemed important that in this branch of science, which has nothing national in it, terms should be found that could go easily into any language, as being erudite rather than popular.[1] I have renounced the advantages of a pleasing style to obtain the greater advantage of scientific treatment. My aim is with clearness and certainty to reconstruct the ideas at the bottom of the prevailing rules and ordinances about money.

I am sorry that I am not able to enter into the merits of my predecessors, Richard Hildebrand, Ignaz Gruber, Karl Knies, Lexis and Bamberger, and many others. To write a full literature of the subject would be a special historical work in itself.

I am making a first sketch, which others must complete.

My heaviest debt is to G. Th. Fechner, who never wrote a line on currency, and indeed knew nothing about it. From him, for example, from his little book on the Soul,[2] we learn how to distinguish the essential from the accidental, and, if anyone says that my own aim has been to discover the soul of money, well, so be it.

Strassburg,
July 5th, 1905.

---

[1] They will be found to be usually Greek, occasionally Latin, as in Chemistry and Botany (Tr.).

[2] *Ueber die Seelenfrage,* Leipzig, 1861.

NOTE BY TRANSLATORS

THE present is an abridged version of Prof. Knapp's book. For reasons of cost the translation has been confined for the present to the theoretical part; and Prof. Knapp's illustrations have been considerably abridged, while every effort has been made to preserve his essential arguments.

To show the scope of the whole book, translated and untranslated, we have given the "Contents" in the complete form, including Chapter IV and the Appendices, which are here omitted.

CONTENTS

CHAPTER I

PAYMENT, MONEY AND METAL

piece should be valid. From the two together follows the *specific* content of the piece.

If the law lays it down that a certain metal may be physically converted into money *without limit*, this is a *genetic* relation between money and metal. We call this metal hylic. The *hylogenic* norm lays down how many units of value in money are to be produced from a unit of weight of the given metal. If this conversion takes place by means of free coinage, and if the content of the piece answers to the norm, we have *specie* money. All other is *notal*, whether coins or paper money pure and simple.

Sometimes a fixed price is obtained for silver or for gold by arrangements which we call *hylodromic*. This is always done by means of two measures, maintenance of a lower limit of price (*hylolepsy*) and of an upper limit (*hylophantism*). No material has *per se* a fixed price. Origin of hylodromy, a useful but not an essential arrangement for currency.

CHAPTER II

CURRENCY WITHIN THE HOME COUNTRY

State money may be recognised by the fact that it is accepted in payment by the State. Classification of payments : (*a*) to the State, (*b*) by the State, and (*c*) other payments, *i. e. epicentric, apocentric* and *paracentric* payments.

In accordance with the regulations as to legal tender, money is divided into *current money*, purely *facultative* money, and *small change money*. There must be at least one *definitive* kind of money, *i. e.* which the creditor must take without being legally entitled to receive other kinds of money for it. There are also provisional kinds of money, legally convertible into definitive money.

The definitive kind of money which the State chooses as final for its own payments and makes compulsory in dubious cases, is called *valuta* money. All other kinds of money are called *accessory*. The valuta money is the " standard," in the narrower sense of the word.

Accessory money comes in freely into the State coffers, is piled up there and often drives out valuta money, because either (1) fresh accessory money is issued, or (2) though accessory is not withdrawn. The second was the case with the thalers and (in France) with the five-franc pieces. To prevent this piling up, free coinage of silver was discontinued in France (1876) and in Austria (1879).

Piling up of accessory money may lead to alteration of standard (*e.g.* led in France to a gold standard, 1860). But the alteration may arise from free choice of the State (as in the German Empire, 1871). The first is an *obstructional* change, the second *exactory*. The change can be *restorative*, when a former standard is restored; or *novatory*, when a new standard is chosen (German in 1871). The change finally can be a rise, a fall, or a poise.

CHAPTER III

MONETARY RELATIONS WITH FOREIGN COUNTRIES

This is a trade phenomenon. The validity of all pieces of money is confined to the State of their origin (unless they are synchartal pieces). Foreign money is a commodity, the price of which is fixed on the Bourse, according to the balance of payment between the States, *i. e.* it is settled *pantopolically*. A Mint parity between the money of different States, where it occurs at all, is used as a standard for the normal exchange parity. In its absence a normal exchange parity is assumed. If the foreign money has a higher value than this, it has an *inter-valutary agio* which must be carefully distinguished from the internal agio of accessory money.

Gold and silver have intrinsically no fixed ratio. London silver prices depend on the balance of payment between the gold standard country, England, and the foreign countries with a silver standard, especially India.

b

CHAPTER IV[1]

HISTORICAL REVIEW OF THE SEVERAL STATES

---

[1] Not here translated.

THE STATE THEORY OF MONEY

CHAPTER I

PAYMENT, MONEY AND METAL

§ 1. *Autometallism ; Nominality of the Unit of Value*

MONEY is a creature of law. A theory of money must therefore deal with legal history.

The favourite form of money is specie. As this implies coins, most writers have concluded that currency can be deduced from numismatics. This is a great mistake. The numismatist usually knows nothing of currency, for he has only to deal with its dead body; he has no ready way to the understanding of paper money pure and simple. It may be a dubious and even dangerous sort of money, but even the worst sort must be included in the theory. Money it must be, in order to be bad money.

Nothing is further from our wishes than to seem to recommend paper money pure and simple in such a form, for instance, as the Austrian State Notes of 1866. It is well for any State to wish to keep to specie money and to have the power to do so. And I know no reason why under normal circumstances we should depart from the gold standard. I say this at once to reassure the public man. Still, in this book

B

the silver standard too is carefully studied, and we have paid more attention to paper money than has been its lot hitherto. For on close consideration it appears that in this dubious form of " degenerate " money lies the clue to the nature of money, paradoxical as this may at first sound. The soul of currency is not in the material of the pieces, but in the legal ordinances which regulate their use.

All money, whether of metal or of paper, is only a special case of the means of payment in general. In legal history the concept of the means of payment is gradually evolved, beginning from simple forms and proceeding to the more complex. There are means of payment which are not yet money; then those which are money; later still those which have ceased to be money.

What then is a means of payment? Is there a wider concept under which means of payment can be subsumed?

Usually, "means of payment" are explained by recourse to the concept "exchange-commodity," which presupposes the concepts "commodity" and "exchange."

In defining one must start from some fixed point. We will venture to regard "commodity" and "exchange" as sufficiently elementary ideas.

If we assert, "Every means of payment is an exchange commodity," we are altogether wrong, for in the course of history we meet with means of payment which are not in any way commodities of exchange in the proper sense of the term. "Exchange-commodity" is therefore not the wider concept we are seeking.

If, however, we say conversely, "Every exchange-commodity is a means of payment," we have not got what we wanted. There are exchange-commodities which are not means of payment.

If one man exchanges corn for another's silver, the silver is an exchange-commodity for the one, corn an exchange-commodity for the other, within this one transaction.

In this wide sense the concept "Exchange-commodity" does not yet serve our purpose; it remains uncertain whether the exchange-commodity is a means of payment. And this cannot be asserted either of silver or of corn, so long as we look only to one transaction.

When, however, in any society, for example, a State, it is a custom gradually recognised by law that all goods should be exchanged against definite quantities of a given commodity, *e. g.* silver, then in this instance silver has become an exchange-commodity in a narrower sense. It is called, therefore, within the range of its use, a general exchange-commodity. The general exchange-commodity is, accordingly, an institution of social intercourse; it is a commodity which has obtained a special use in society, first by custom, then by law.

Such a " socially " recognised exchange-commodity is, of course, always a means of payment, and therefore is included in the concept " means of payment." On the other hand, it is untrue that every means of payment is a socially recognised exchange-commodity. It is indeed always socially recognised and also is always used for exchange; but it is questionable whether it is always a commodity. In order to be a commodity it must, in addition to its use in the manner provided by law, also be capable of a use in the world of art and industry, and this is not the case with all means of payment. The sheets of paper, which are all the eye of the craftsman sees in paper money, are an example of an object which has no other industrial use. They are therefore not an exchange-commodity, though they are a means of exchange.

The result of our considerations, cautiously stated as theory demands, is as follows. In the socially recognised exchange-commodity we have an instance of a means of payment, and therefore not its definition; it is only a special case of a means of payment, and that the simplest that can be imagined. Let us assume that this exchange-commodity consists of a metal—which is not absolutely necessary, but occurs in the most important case—we can then give a name to this simplest form of the means of payment; it is " autometallistic."

Autometallism views metal only as material and

gives no juristic consideration to the form of the pieces. The quantity of the material is measured in a merely physical manner; in the case of a metal, by weighing. The exchange-commodity is always weighed out to the creditor.

There is no difficulty in conceiving autometallism; the only difficulty is with those means of payment which are no longer autometallistic (*e. g.* money). We shall therefore use autometallism in order to show what is the distinguishing characteristic of the concept "means of payment." Let us put ourselves in the place of the creditor. A man receiving a pound of silver (or copper or gold) in exchange for commodities, which are not means of payment, can use it in two ways. Either he can use the silver in some craft to make vessels such as goblets or plates, or perhaps even rings and chains for ornament, or else he can use it as a means of exchange, and obtain with it other commodities as he needs them. The holder can make use of his property in one of these two ways, but not in both at once. He can either use it in some craft, thus obtaining "real" satisfaction, or else obtain other commodities with it, when his satisfaction is derived from its value in exchange.

The possibility of "real" satisfaction is undoubtedly a necessary condition for any commodity becoming a socially recognised exchange-commodity. If metals had not been indispensable in handicrafts, autometallism would never have arisen. But there

is " real " satisfaction in every commodity which is
taken in exchange. A man who barters a sheep for
wooden dishes, takes the dishes only because they
give real satisfaction, *i. e.* because he can use them.
But the dishes do not thereby become socially recognised exchange-commodities. The possibility of
" real " use is therefore essential if a commodity (*e. g.*
a metal) is to be chosen as a socially recognised exchange-commodity; but this property is insufficient
to make it a means of payment.

With the satisfaction derived from exchange [1] the
position is quite different. It is a necessary and
sufficient property of every means of payment, and
of the autometallistic in particular. A man who can
employ the exchange-commodity he has received for
some craft, but cannot pass it on in circulation, owns
a commodity, but not a means of payment. For
example, the owner of a pound of copper would be
in this position if in his country silver was the
autometallistic means of payment.

It is of the greatest importance that this should be
borne in mind. Even in autometallism (the simplest
form of a means of payment) it is first the possibility
of employing it in exchange that gives it the property
of becoming a means of payment. The possibility of
" real " use does not produce this property, otherwise all goods would be already potentially means of
payment, for they all have a technical use.

---

[1] " Circulatory satisfaction."

The use in exchange is a legal phenomenon. Even autometallism is therefore a legal form of the means of payment.

Let us not forget, however, that autometallism is only one instance of means of payment.

Whenever a material, measured in some physical manner, is used as a recognised exchange-commodity, we will call this form *authylic* (*hyle* meaning matter). Autometallism is only the most important example of *authylism*; and authylism itself is only one instance of a means of payment, an instance, namely, where the holder can choose between " real " satisfaction and " circulatory."

What then is a means of payment? A movable object which can in any case be used for circulation. This, however, is a mere general hint, and you will please note that "real" use should not come into the definition. It would be equally wrong either to demand or to exclude it.

It is difficult to give a correct definition of a means of payment, just as in mathematics we cannot say what a line or a number is, or in zoology define an animal. Often the simplest case (straight line, positive integer) is taken, and one can then proceed to widen the concept, at first recognised in a given example.

Suppose we said, " A means of payment is a movable thing which has the legal property of being the bearer of units of value," this would be exactly what we mean.

But let us not give this as a definition, for it would assume "unit of value" as a self-evident notion, which it is far from being.

Let us say no more than is absolutely necessary for our purpose. First, the unit of value is nothing but the unit in which the amount of the payment is expressed. Every traveller entering a new country asks the name of this unit—whether accounts are in marks, francs, crowns or sterling. When this question is answered, the traveller asks what the usual means of payment look like and what they are worth in the unit of that country. He is then in a position to make payments himself. We see that the unit of value has everywhere a name which in some countries has remained unaltered for centuries (pound sterling), while in others (*e. g.* Austria) it has been deliberately changed (to krone since 1892). In any case there is a name, and the question is now what it means.

Can it be defined according to its technical use (that is, use in a craft)? For example, a mark is the $\frac{1}{1395}$th part of a pound of gold. The metallists would so define it.

Or is it absolutely impossible to define by technical use? If so, in what other way are we to define? This is the task of the nominalists.

The metallists tell us we can only speak of the value of a commodity by comparison with another commodity. A man purchasing a commodity says how much of another commodity he is prepared to spend

on it.   A man selling a commodity says how much of
another commodity he will take for it.   Each time
the equivalent is mentioned for comparison, so that
the idea of the value may have only one meaning.
It is equally clear here that the value is a fact which
cannot be determined by observation, but rests on an
agreement.   A third person can, of course, observe
what an object is worth, but only by observing the
agreement of the buyers and sellers.   If the commodity used for comparison is not expressly named,
the value of an object then means the *lytric* value,
that is, the value that results from a comparison with
the universally recognised means of exchange.   From
this, again, it follows that we cannot in this sense
speak of the value of the means of exchange itself.
Only those commodities have lytric value which are
not themselves means of exchange.

The metallist always conceives a means of exchange
to be an exchange-commodity.

All these propositions are indubitably correct.
It follows that the concept of lytric value can only
arise from a comparison with a generally recognised
exchange-commodity, which, as we have seen, is
always the simplest form of the means of payment.

But there are means of payment which extend
beyond this simple form, namely, those which are
not commodities except in so far as law makes them
so.   The most important case is real genuine paper
money.   The name of the unit of value (*e. g.* gulden,

in Austria) continues to exist, but it is no longer possible to give it a technical definition such as " a gulden is the $\frac{1}{45}$th part of a pound of silver," for it is plain to anyone that this is indeed a definition of a gulden of sorts, not of that gulden in which payments are made, but of a kind of gulden in which no one pays. What we must define is the unit of the customary means of payment, and this is impossible for the metallist in the case before us.

We have now reached the point where opinions differ. As long as autometallism prevails, the technical definition of the unit of value can be quietly accepted, at any rate as long as the metal once chosen is retained unaltered. The man in the street is, however (in secret and quite unconsciously), of the opinion that we still have autometallism, only slightly altered and rendered more convenient by coining. Hence the wide acceptance of the view that we can define the unit of value as a given quantity of metal.

The natural man is a metallist; the theorist, on the other hand, is forced to become a nominalist, because it is not always possible to define the unit of value as a given quantity of metal.

It cannot be done in the instance, already mentioned, of genuine paper money. Another fact, however, is more astonishing—it cannot be done at all when the means of payment are money, which is not yet the case with autometallism. But the strangest fact of all is this. Even in the case of autometallism, as soon as another metal is chosen, the concept of the unit of value becomes independent of the former metal, *i. e.* technically independent of it. For the unit of value is always a historical concept.

The fact of the existence of debts gives the reason why it is not always possible to define the unit of value technically, but is always possible to define it historically.

Our theorists are inclined to think of payment as immediate; the craftsman supposes that coin is handed over in exchange for a given weight of silver. But, if payment has not been made on the spot, there are certain permanent obligations to pay, that is, debts. The State, as the maintainer of law, adopts a definite attitude to this phenomenon, which is not technical but juristic. Through its Courts of Law the State gives a right of action for debt. We are speaking here only of debts which are expressed in units of value (sterling, marks, roubles), yet not merely of those under the ruling monetary system, but of lytric debts generally, so that in times of autometallism we include debts expressed in pounds of copper or pounds of silver.

Debts which are expressed in units of value and are discharged with a means of payment (*lytron*) will be called *lytric* debts.

In what then does a lytric debt consist—especially in the case of autometallism, and, more generally, in the case of authylism?

In the case of authylism the unit of value is named in terms of the material composing it. As everyone knows wheat or rye, copper or silver, and the meaning of a bushel or a pound, there is no uncertainty as to the means of payment. A lytric debt is defined by means of this well-known concept. A man is bound to hand over so much corn, when corn is used for payment, or so much copper when that is in question, and if we at first regard the material of payment as invariable.

As the thing which serves as a means of payment according to existing laws is technically defined, it can be said in the case of authylism that lytric debts are " real debts." For the material in which the debtor is bound to discharge his debt can always be named.

If the law remains unchanged, the lytric system ends here; further development is excluded; money cannot come into being. In that case, if autometallism had begun with copper, we should still have autometallism in copper, and scales would be an indispensable adjunct for payments.

This obviously is not so, and the course of history shows that the State as lawgiver must certainly take up an attitude towards existing debts quite different from that we have here imagined.

This view is not easy for the jurist, as he is accustomed to take as his starting-point an existing state of law, which is in his eyes unalterable. The legal historian, on the other hand, will adjust himself to the position more easily.

In the case of autometallism, if the material, once chosen, remains unaltered, the principle is maintained that debts should remain unaltered.

Now almost everybody thinks that it is a legal principle that the absolute amount of debts judged according to the original material used in payment should remain unaltered. Historical experience, however, teaches quite a different lesson. The State always maintains only the relative amount of debts, while it alters the means of payment from time to time. Sometimes it even does this while it is still in the state of autometallism, by introducing a different metal from the one previously employed for lytric use. If the State declares silver to be the material for payment instead of copper, the relative amount of the existing debts remains unaltered, but anyone might think that, judged on the old basis of copper, the debts have changed.

The proceeding we mean is the alteration of the means of payment by the introduction of a new commodity for payment in place of the old one. Two epochs are separated from one another by the moment in which the State declares that payments shall no longer be made by weighing out copper, but by weighing out silver. This causes a most remarkable change in the debts arising in the earlier period. They are incurred in pounds of copper—the State declares that they are repayable in some ounces of silver. It lays down the ratio of silver to a pound of copper, regulating the amount perhaps according to the price of silver on that day in the older means of payment, copper.

The State therefore treats the older debts as if the unit of value, a pound of copper, were only a name by the use of which the relative amount of the debt was indicated, and which does not mean that in reality copper was to be delivered. The State reserves to itself the right to order that " a pound of copper " should now mean that a given weight of silver was to be paid.

At the moment of transition from copper to silver, the State treats existing debts as nominal debts and immediately adds what other material, and how much of it, shall in future represent the unit of the means of payment.

While, therefore, most people believe that in the case of previously existing debts the State recognises the continuance of the former means of payment, legal history shows that all the State recognises is the relative amount of the old debt, and says that it will alter the means of payment from time to time. Or, in actual fact, the State says nothing, but acts; the legal historian, however, calls the State's action frankly by its proper name.

The State accordingly regards the former unit of payment (a pound of copper) as if it meant only the

name of the former unit without attaching any importance to the material of which it was composed.   On
the other hand, it recognises that all old debts are
uniformly to be converted into debts in the new means
of payment.

Lytric debts are, therefore, from the State's point
of view, debts which are to be discharged in the means
of payment for the time being.   If the State alters
the means of payment, it lays down a rule for the
conversion of the one into the other.   The new means
of payment must therefore refer back to the old one.
It is only this reference that makes it possible to carry
on business in the new means of payment, because
at the moment of change care must be taken that
the old debts should not lapse, but be able to be
discharged.

Lytric debts under autometallism are therefore
" real " debts as long as the material for payment
remains the same.   As, however, the introduction of
another means of payment is from the State's point
of view possible, they are in that case " *nominal* "
debts.

"*Nominal* " debts are debts repayable in the means
of payment current at the time.   Their amount in the
units of value then in use is calculated in relation to the
earlier unit.

The State, therefore, conceives lytric debts not as
" real debts " in the material for payment which was
in use when the debt was incurred, but as nominal

debts repayable in the material in use at the time of repayment.

Such "nominal debts" are not really indefinite. All that is indefinite is the material in which they are discharged.

Considered from the point of view of legal history, lytric debts are therefore always "nominal" debts, *i. e.* they refer at first to the lytric unit at the time they are incurred; but should the means of payment change they are converted into debts in the new lytric unit. They therefore do not depend on the old means of payment, but on the relation of the new unit of value to the old.

The nominality of lytric debts, as a matter of legal history, is clearly seen, even under autometallism, though of course only at the moment when the State institutes a change in the material of payment. Old debts must in any case be maintained. Consequently the nominality of lytric debts exists already even where both the old and the new means of payment are defined entirely in terms of material. The nominality of the debts is therefore not inconsistent with the material nature of the means of payment, but only with its immutability. As soon as the material of payment can be changed, lytric debts are "nominal."

For a long time I shrank from recognising that the nominal unit of value was quite sufficient for judging the lytric value of commodities—I made the same mistake as almost everybody else. I thought that judgments of value could only be made by comparison of commodities between themselves. Now, however, all we can say is that the first judgments of value came about in that way. But, when once this form of judgment has become habitual, the comparison of commodity with commodity is unnecessary, for judgments as to the value of a given commodity can be given in terms of the nominal unit of value, which is only defined historically. I must refer anyone who doubts this to the historical development of lytric dealings. Such phenomena as genuine paper money actually exist, and are only possible, if we assume nominal units of value. The nominality of the unit of value, therefore, is established by experience like the facts of the legal development of lytric institutions.

This, however, must not be taken to be a defence of such a lytric form as is only adequate for home business; for example, genuine paper money.

Nothing prevents us from developing the lytric form, so that, if need be, it can afford " real " satisfaction, and then, in addition to its use at home, facilitate dealings abroad.

All this can come about while the unit of value is " nominal," for there is no necessary contradiction.

Now when the State alters the means of payment, though at first still within the limits of authylism (that is, by the introduction of a new material in place of the old), does anyone lose ? Of course ; and why not,

C

if the State has paramount reasons for its actions?
It can never gain its ends without damage to
certain private interests. What interests these are
we will illustrate by the transition from copper to
silver.

A man who in former times produced copper by
mining had straightway means of payment in hand
—from a commercial point of view, an enviable position. Now he must first bring his copper to market
as a commodity in order to buy silver, the new
commodity for payment.

The man who formerly used copper as raw material
for the production of weapons had a fixed price for it.
Now he has to buy his raw material as a commodity,
for he must offer silver for it.

On the other hand, the owner of silver mines is
now in the favoured position that his produce is now
straightway a means of payment, and the man who
works up silver into vessels or ornaments can now get
his material at a fixed price, for he takes it from the
new means of payment now in circulation.

All these are disturbances of existing interests.

But now we turn to the large group of the " neutral "
inhabitants of the State, that is, to those who neither
now nor before produced the material for payment
nor yet consumed it, e. g. worked it up as raw material.
For the group of neutrals the change in the material
of payment is unimportant.

They now pay their debts in silver instead of in

copper, but they also receive what is owed to them in silver instead of in copper. Neutrals are only concerned with the lytric aspect of these two metals, and consequently they make little or no resistance.

Thus a change in the material for payment causes but little disturbance. If the new material is easier to handle than the old, almost everyone is pleased with the change and it soon seems quite natural.

The nominality of debts does not lie in the fact that the State alters the means of payment more or less often, but in the fact that such an alteration is possible in principle, whether it is made or not. The nominality of debts and of the unit of value is a necessary premise before money can come into being. Money is a means of payment, but not necessarily a material one. It is therefore in any case a differently constituted means of payment from the purely material one of authylism.

Each alteration of the means of payment implies that the unit of value, at least at the moment of transition, should be regarded as " nominal."

The nominality of the unit of value, and therefore of lytric debts, is not a new, but a very old phenomenon which still exists to-day and which will continue for ever. It is compatible with any form of the means of payment, and is nothing but the necessary condition for progress from one means of payment to another.

It only remains unnoticed in periods when the means of payment do not change. From the temporary constancy of the means of payment, people draw the false conclusion of immutability.

The permanent element in lytric debts is then not the means of payment, but the principle that these debts expressed in old units of value are all convertible into the new units in such a way that their relative size remains unaltered.

In the authylistic, and especially in the autometallistic system, there is usually no proper name for the unit of value. The designation " a pound of copper " or a pound of silver is ambiguous, so that it remains uncertain whether a " real " debt or a " nominal " debt is meant. A man using copper or silver for a craft will regard such debts as " real " debts and will demand that the material named should be delivered. A man, however, who sees in silver or copper only the means of payment then current, will expect that at a later time the debt should be discharged in the equivalent means of payment. How is this difficulty to be settled ? It has been settled long ago, for the State has adopted *de facto* without conscious intention the following presumption.

A debt expressed in quantities of a material which, at the time it was incurred, was a means of payment, is a nominal lytric debt. If a " real " debt is meant, this must be explicitly stated. If it is not, the debt is nominal. In doubtful cases the nominality of lytric debts is presupposed by the State.

This action of the State as maintainer of law does not appear with the creation of money, *e. g.* with the coining of lytric metal or the introduction of independent paper money, but at the first time of alteration in the means of payment. Before that there were no grounds for deciding the question of " nominality " or " reality."

As soon as the State introduces a new means of payment in the place of the old, the law (1) should so describe the new means of payment that it should be immediately recognisable. (2) The law should settle a name for the new unit of value and call the new means of payment by it. By this means the validity (*Geltung*) of the new means of payment is established in units of value. (3) The unit of value which is to come into use is defined by its relation to the previous unit. It is therefore historically defined.

In general there is no other definition of the new unit of value. The historical definition signifies that so many of the new units represented in the new means of payment are legally valid for the discharge of an existing debt in the old unit.

The definition of the new unit therefore consists in the declaration as to how many new units are legally equivalent to one old unit. This definition has absolutely nothing to do with the material in which the old means of payment consisted, nor yet the new. It only contains the proportion of the new to the old unit of value, *i. e.* it relates the new unit back to the old one.

All this had already happened in the epoch of autometallism. Let us assume that the transition has been made from copper to silver; the process will be as follows.

First, the State describes the new means of payment by saying it shall consist of the metal silver.

Secondly, the State ordains that the new unit shall be called a " pound of silver," and for the description of the new means of payment it lays down the rule in this special instance, that it shall be formed by the physical experiment of weighing. Each quantity of silver is called legally as many " pounds of silver " as it weighs pounds.

Thirdly, the State says that the unit " pound of silver " takes the place of so many earlier units, *e. g.* fifty pounds of copper. That is the legal definition of the new unit.

As soon as all this has been done, the transition from copper to silver is complete.

It is frequently overlooked that autometallism already possesses a name for the unit of value. It always coincides with the unit of weight of the material, but it is still there. The characteristic of autometallism is not that it has no name, but that it has no special one, and, what is much more important,

autometallism has the rule that the denomination of
the means of payment in units (that is, the lytric
denomination) should be found by the physical
experiment of weighing. But it is not true, and
would entirely destroy the generality of the theory,
if we say that the denomination of a means of payment is determined in accordance with the result of
weighing. That is only in a given instance. In
general the lytric name is not subject to this rule, but
is an authoritative act of law.

Many people think—to continue with our example
—that the back-reference of the unit " pound of
silver " to the earlier unit " pound of copper " is
regulated according to the prevailing price of silver
expressed in copper.

This makes the transaction easier for those people
who can only conceive the material for payment as a
commodity. But it is not essential to the reference.
For one thing, there are transitions from one means
of payment to another where such consideration of
the price is out of the question. In its broadest aspect
the reference back to the earlier unit is in every case,
like the name of the unit of value, an authoritative
act of law, which may or may not follow such a
rule.

Finally, it is correct to say that in the example
chosen above, both the old unit of value, " a pound of
copper," and the new, " a pound of silver," can be
presented in a " real " form, for the example is drawn

from autometallism. But presentation in a " real " form is always a special case, which is possible but not necessary. If this is forgotten, the most important transitions, which we shall consider later, are incomprehensible.

The following general principles remain :

(1) The choice of the means of payment is a free act of the State's authority.

(2) The denomination of the means of payment according to new units of value is a free act of the State's authority.

(3) The definition of the new unit is also a free act of the State's authority.

Just because these acts are free, they may or may not follow special rules.

This view excludes the idea that the " real " form of the unit of value is the rule and its absence the exception; that, as a rule, the denomination is given by weight, and that the reference of the new unit back to the old one is settled according to the level of price.

Only a very imperfect logic can speak so. Here the question is not of what happens in most cases and of what is only rarely absent; we want to get at the essence of the matter—the actual general statement which does not admit of exceptions but only of special cases.

In the interest of the universality of our theory we are compelled to say that the validity of our means of

payment is not bound to its material content, and that
the unit of value is only defined historically.

§ 2. *Chartal Means of Payment*

We observed the fact that in human society a
definite commodity, or, more accurately, a definite
material grew into a means of payment. Then we
saw that the notion of a means of payment is not
bound to a particular material. Hence the concept,
means of payment, is freed from the actual nature of
the material, *e. g.* is indifferently copper or silver, but
remains bound to the condition that there should be
some material. This is as far as one can get by an
examination of autometallism. The unit of value is
no longer definitely " real," but it is so indefinitely,
no longer a pound of copper or an ounce of silver, but
always a given quantity of a material prescribed by
law, whether copper or silver or gold. Debts in units
of value—lytric debts—are debts repayable in the
material used in payments at the time, even if they
were contracted in another material.

As long, therefore, as this lytric system lasts, nominality is a property of lytric debts. Under autometallism there are no means of payment other than metal,
though the decision what metal is to be used for payment is the business of legal regulation. This choice
of the metal by the law is here the only sign of
nominality. So long as a given material is *per se* a

means of payment, money has not yet come into being.

The question is now whether the means of payment can reach a still higher stage of development; whether a state of things is conceivable in which the means of payment is something other than a material selected for this purpose.

As the first means of payment are movable objects, and as movable objects cannot be thought of apart from matter, of course no means of payment is conceivable which does not consist in matter. The question is, therefore, not whether there might conceivably be immaterial means of payment, but whether there could be means of payment which are defined otherwise than pensatorially, by the weight of a particular material.

There must obviously be something of the kind, for it is common knowledge that in our present lytric systems no payments are made with raw material. To-day, in the countries of our standard of civilisation, it is not possible to pay by weighing out copper or silver or gold.

We always pay in " pieces," *i. e.* in movable objects which are defined not by their matter but by their form. We pay, therefore, in shaped movable objects, and shaped movable objects which bear signs upon them. This is not all; but think for a moment what it means. All coins which we use in payment come under this head, whether formed of precious or of base metal. They are all made of metal, shaped and bearing signs. Sometimes also there are warrants, that is, means of payment which, to the outward eye, consist of writing material, not metal but usually paper. Such warrants are undoubtedly movable, shaped, sign-bearing objects, whatever else they are.

What has been hitherto said about the " pieces " used in payment is insufficient, for we have only spoken of their nature as technical products. It must be added that we pay with pieces that have a legal significance. Our law lays it down that only pieces formed in such and such a manner are to be admitted as means of payment, and the significant marks of the pieces are prescribed by law. In what follows only such pieces are meant.

The means of payment at present in common use always have this form, *i. e.* that of pieces in the legal sense. They are " morphic."

Morphic means of payment are, as we shall see, not always money, but all money comes under the head of morphic means of payment. *Morphism* is a necessary, but is not a far-reaching, condition for a system of money.

The morphic form is no longer authylistic, for authylism is from a legal point of view amorphic. It admits pieces which, technically considered, have forms and signs, but these forms and signs have no significance in law. As soon as the forms and signs are significant for delimiting what is a means of payment and what is not, we have morphism.

Authylism has still another property—measurement by weighing, which in the case of autometallism gains a legal significance. There is nothing here contradictory to morphism, though morphism tries to make weighing superfluous.

It is important to be clear on this point. There can be morphic means of payment the validity of which at the time of payment is established by weighing; in the language of the Bourse this use is *al marco*, by weight. As we should express it, these are morphic means of payment with pensatory practice.

We do not mean by this that the pieces are weighed out when they are struck, for this happens in the case of all our coins. *Ponderal* production—production according to weight—means a weighing which precedes the act of payment. Pensatory practice, on the other hand, means the practice of weighing at the time of payment in order to establish the validity. Since there is such a thing as a wearing down of the pieces, it is necessary to keep the two distinct.

Let us suppose, for example, that the familiar gold coins called ducats are introduced as the means of payment. When they are struck, the discs are weighed out; there is ponderal production. Suppose it is laid down that the ducats are to be used for payment according to the weight which they actually have; this is pensatory practice. The unit of value would be in that case, by our own system of weights, the gramme of ducat gold, *i. e.* not any gramme of gold of the fineness prescribed for the coining of ducats, for that would be autometallism, but the gramme of gold coined into ducat form. The gramme of gold in this form is a totally different concept from the gramme of gold of which ducats could be made.

Such a system is conceivable. It would produce a pensatory morphic means of payment, and the wearing down of the pieces, so long as they were still recognisable as ducats, would be quite unimportant, because the ducats were valid " al marco." On the other hand, mere payment by counting would be excluded, because there would probably be many worn pieces. The gold scales must always be held in readiness.

As is well known, we have no such system in modern civilised States. We are most careful to avoid pensatory practice, because the aim of all modern monetary systems is to discard the scales as an instrument of payment. Mere morphism does not yet bring this about, for the ducat system we have described above is unquestionably already morphic, though it still remains pensatory.

Is there then another method of settling the validity of the pieces besides weighing? Certainly, as soon as there is a morphic monetary system.

Morphism gives the possibility of recognising the means of payment without the necessity, which

previously existed, of naming any given substance, for
the legal ordinances describe the permissible pieces
explicitly.   When legal ordinances give the name to
the unit of value (as mark, franc or rouble) and define
it by reference to the earlier unit, there is nothing to
prevent us from giving to the morphic means of payment a validity dependent not on weight but on fiat.
A proclamation is made that a piece of such and such
a description shall be valid as so many units of value.
Morphism therefore opens a way which is not pensatory.   The validity can depend on proclamation.
This means the final abolition of the scales for the act
of payment.   Moreover, the wearing down of the
pieces is of no importance so long as they are still
recognisable.

Validity by proclamation is commonly called the
" face value," in contrast with the " intrinsic value "
of the pieces, which is supposed to depend on their
metallic content.   This is a habit of the metallists,
who are always autometallists at heart.

Validity by proclamation is not bound to any
material.   It can occur with the most precious or the
basest metals, and in all cases where payments are
not pensatory, *i. e.* in all modern monetary systems.
Moreover, as we have seen, we should not apply the
concept " value " to this means of payment, and therefore not to this money itself, but only to things which
are not means of payment, for in the case of " value "
we always use the current means of payment as a

standard of comparison; but do not refer back to the
autometallistic form, for it is precisely the overcoming
of autometallism that we are depicting.

Settling the validity by proclamation is therefore
not inconsistent with the contents of the pieces being
of a given quality, but it is inconsistent with the pensatory definition of the validity.   In modern monetary
systems proclamation is always supreme.   The fact
that the pieces are of a given content may have all
sorts of results, but it is not the basis of the validity.
It is so only when payment remains pensatory, a
case so rare that we had to invent our example of the
ducats.   There are, however, pensatory reactions so
important that we had to admit this form into
our system in order to be able to refer to it on
occasion.

As a set off to " pensatory " we need another short
name for " morphic proclamatory " means of payment,
the metallic contents of which are of no importance for
validity.   At least they are movable objects which
have in law a significance independent of their substance.   Law offers many such objects in ordinary
life.   When we give up our coats in the cloak-room of
a theatre, we receive a tin disc of a given size bearing
a sign, perhaps a number.   There is nothing more on
it, but this ticket or mark has legal significance; it is
a proof that I am entitled to demand the return of
my coat.

When we send letters, we affix a stamp or ticket

which proves that we have by payment of postage obtained the right to get the letter carried.

The " ticket " is then a good expression, which has long since been naturalised, for a movable, shaped object bearing signs, to which legal ordinance gives a use independent of its material.

Our means of payment, then, whether coins or warrants, possess the above-named qualities : they are pay-tokens, or tickets used as means of payment.

The idea of the ticket or token tells us nothing as to the material of the disc. It is made both of precious and of base metal and also of paper, to mention only the most important. Let it not be thought, therefore, that a ticket or token means an object made of a worthless material, compared with the autometallistic means of payment which preceded it. The value of the disc is left unconsidered for the present. It is only necessary that we recognise this sign-bearing object as a legal non-pensatory means of payment.

Perhaps the Latin word " Charta " can bear the sense of ticket or token, and we can form a new but intelligible adjective—" Chartal." Our means of payment have this token, or Chartal, form.

Among civilised peoples in our day, payments can only be made with pay-tickets or Chartal pieces.

The chartality of the means of payment would never disappear even if coins should be totally abolished, which in view of their convenience for small payments is not likely.

It is important that these tokens should bear signs exactly described by legal ordinance. It is not important that they should bear any written inscription. The letters or hieroglyphics (coats of arms) are of no consequence. They are significant merely as a means of identification. The meaning is to be found out not by reading the signs, but by consulting the legal ordinances.

Coins bearing both the arms of the Austrian State and the effigy of the Austrian Emperor can, accordingly, cease to be Austrian means of payment as soon as the Austrian legal ordinances command that they should. But the very same coins, in spite of their foreign imprint, can be means of payment in the German Empire (*e. g.* the Austrian *Vereinsthaler*) because German law so ordains. This is no imaginary instance, but until 1900 was a well-known fact.

The legal significance of Chartal means of payment is not, therefore, to be known from the pieces themselves. The piece has on it mere signs to be interpreted by Acts of Parliament or other sources of law.

Objects thus inscribed could be called " symbols," if this phrase did not suggest the wrong idea that such means of payment are there simply to recall others better and more genuine, without being themselves either good or genuine.

In the first place among " Chartal " means of pay-

D

ment are many which leave nothing to be desired in the matter of genuineness and goodness, even from the standpoint of the strictest metallism, such as our own gold pieces. Secondly, the warrants or notes, which are no less Chartal, also contain much that is good and genuine, though in a field less familiar to the metallists. For these reasons it is inconvenient to speak of symbolic means of payment, especially as people would understand this in the purely negative sense of autometallistic if they had that term.

This, however, has never been clearly stated, for the expression autometallism has not been current hitherto.

In the case of *Chartality* the pieces are regarded as something one and indivisible, as objective individuals.

Chartality and pensatory practice are mutually exclusive, like morphism and amorphism.

The chartality of the means of payment is not a question of technique; only the production of shaped pieces, which we call morphism, is technical, and the first kind of morphism is the production of coins in their earliest form.

Chartality rests on a certain relation to the laws. It is, therefore, impossible to tell from the pieces themselves whether they are Chartal or not. This is at once evident in the case of warrants. As to coins, we must always refer to the Acts and statutes, which alone can give information.

Now while morphism originates in a technical invention—the coining of the metal which was formerly used by weight—Chartality has come in unperceived, so completely unperceived that hitherto it has not even had a name.

What happened was this : When shaped pieces were first coined, the chief consideration was that it should be possible to recognise immediately the nature and quantity of the metal, which had formerly been used by weight. This was in order to make it unnecessary to examine or weigh the material. At first no one thought of the wearing down of the pieces. It was therefore unnecessary to consider whether the use of the pieces was to depend on weighing or proclamation, for when the pieces are intact the distinction is useless.

As, however, in course of time the wearing down of the pieces became noticeable, the question arose, which causes uncertainty even in modern times : "Are the pieces valid in accordance with their weight?" If the answer is yes, pensatory payment still continues; but if the pieces gain their validity through proclamation, they are Chartal.

Chartality, then, is simply the use in accordance with proclamation of certain means of payment having a visible shape.

As soon as the legal property of chartality has arisen, this makes possible another development, at which we have hitherto only hinted.

Authylism—and, consequently, its most usual form, autometallism—always presupposes that there is a material for payment. The means of payment are therefore in this system always *hylogenic*, as we call this property.

It is already there in the material. It does not come about through the material alone; but emerges only through a particular use of the material.

Once the concept of chartability has come into being, the possibility for the first time arises of means of payment which are no longer hylogenic, and which we will call *autogenic*. Autogenic means of payment need not necessarily arise at this point, but they may do so and cannot do so before. For chartality makes the material contents of the pieces a concomitant circumstance, which perhaps may have important effects, but which is no longer essential to establish the validity of the coin.

In the authylic form the material is all-important, for the description of what is to be a means of payment consists, and can only at this stage consist, in a statement of the material.

This is all, and it is not at that stage possible to imagine any other means of recognition.

When, however, chartality has developed, the description of the stamped pieces gives a new method of recognising the means of payment, for the State says that the pieces have such and such an appearance and that their validity is fixed by proclamation.

Here, therefore, it is not the statement of a specific material, but the description of the shaped pieces, which makes the means of payment recognisable.

This being so, the Chartal pieces may still be hylogenic, but they may also be autogenic.

At the beginning people hold fast to the hylogenic tradition, and produce hylogenic Chartal pieces. At a later stage a change is made to means of payment which are no longer hylogenic, and this is made possible by chartality. The reasons for this proceeding are not in place here, and the dangers incidental to it must be discussed elsewhere. All we have to remember is that chartality makes possible autogenic means of payment.

The autogeneity of the means of payment was virtually, though not actually, created at the moment when, through a legal decision, chartality arose. For why should not pieces out of any stuff you please be chartally treated ? If, however, the material can be chosen at will, then the authylic material formerly used may be just as well left in its place as driven from it. Chartality does not demand autogenic means of payment, but admits them as well as the hylogenic.

Grasp the meaning of chartality and you understand hylogenic means of payment just as easily as autogenic.

After this introduction it is easy to answer the great question of lytrology, " What is money ? "

In the German language money (*Geld*) always means a formed (morphic) means of payment; but there are morphic means of payment which nevertheless are pensatory. This, however, is at a lower stage of development which will be outgrown in the course of history. For the more exact observer money in the modern sense first comes into being when the morphic means of payment have their validity settled by proclamation and become Chartal. So we get the following answer to the question we have asked.

Money always signifies a Chartal means of payment. Every Chartal means of payment we call money. The definition of money is therefore " a Chartal means of payment."

But, once money exists, a distinction should be made between the hylogenic and the autogenic.

For many reasons people prefer hylogenic money, but no one denies that there is also autogenic money, for the much-decried inconvertible paper money is still money, and what is it but autogenic money made of paper discs ? Our theory therefore gives even this step-child its due.

The order in which lytric phenomena are dealt with here is not arbitrary but necessary.

(1) We presupposed the hylogenesis of the means of payment, for only hylic means of payment allow of pensatory use. (2) Then morphism appears; only morphic means of payment can be proclamatory and therefore Chartal. (3) Finally, it is only in the case of

Chartal means of payment that the hylic basis can disappear; they alone, therefore, can be autogenic.

Our classification, therefore, of means of payment is not only possible but strictly necessary, as may be seen from the fact that historically the phenomena appear in this order.

The nominality of the unit of value is, as we have seen, created by the State in its capacity as the guardian and maintainer of law. This, however, does not occur through philosophic reflection but quite otherwise. The State sees itself for some reason or other forced to introduce a new means of payment in place of the old, while it wishes to preserve existing debts, at any rate in their relative proportions one to another. Jurisprudence, having to reckon with this fact, now sets reflection to work, and under compulsion proceeds to put the lytric nominal debt in place of the real debt, because in no other way can it accommodate itself to the new situation.

The chartality of the means of payment arises in a similar way. The State as guardian of the law declares that the property of being the means of payment should be inherent in certain stamped pieces as such, and not in the material of the pieces. In this case also juridical reflection goes to work and creates the concept of the pay-token or ticket, not from caprice but because it must accommodate itself to the altered situation. Finally, the same holds good of autogenesis. The State, not the jurist, creates it.

In all these cases the impulse comes from the political action of the State, jurisprudence only drawing its conclusions from the State's action as it needs them.

If we have already declared in the beginning that money is a creation of law, this is not to be interpreted in the narrower sense that it is a creation of jurisprudence, but in the larger sense that it is a creation of the legislative activity of the State, a creation of legislative policy.

The Chartal form does not forbid the use of costly material for the making of means of payment, but, on the other hand, it does not demand it. Chartality makes the concept of the means of payment independent of the material. The Chartal form is the ample frame in which can be set means of payment, whether made of precious material or of the poorest material.

It is not on this account, however, a matter of indifference which case actually occurs. The nature of the material has its special effects, to which we will devote our attention in the proper place. Here it is only important to establish what the nature of the Chartal form is, leaving aside for the present the question as to what qualities are inherent in the different kinds of Chartal constitution.

From what we have said it appears that the Chartal form is associated with the State which introduces it, for the use of the piece must take place where the law runs, *i. e.* it is limited to the State's territory, for the

law does not operate beyond its boundaries. The
Chartal form can never be effective " internation-
ally," or, rather, it can never be effective from State
to State, as long as States are totally independent of
one another.

This is a striking limitation of it, compared with
autometallism.

If two States have the same autometallism, that
is, both pay in copper or both in silver, in that case
they have at once an international (better, inter-
political) means of payment. This form of common
system is excluded by the idea of the Chartal constitution. If two States should make an agreement for
pooling their money, then for our purposes they are
no longer separate States, but form a community of
States which is to be regarded as a whole.

The question, therefore, why we have no inter-
political money in the countries of our civilisation is
easily answered. It is because the Chartal form prevails everywhere, and this essentially excludes the
idea that there should be a money common to two
independent States.

The person who demands inter-political money
opposes the Chartal form, with small prospects of
success. If he fixes his hopes on unions, let him
remember that States have to care for other things
besides currency.

Of course such supplements could be made to
the Chartal system that the chief ends of an

" international " monetary system could be attained, by roundabout methods, of which we will speak later. It is a completely perverted idea to demand " international " money for independent States which are not even allied. On the other hand, it is always permissible to wish for monetary arrangements which hinder international dealings as little as possible.

The " genetic " division of means of payment results from what we have said. We call that division " genetic " when we only take account of those circumstances which are characteristic of its origin. At this point be it assumed that the State only admits one kind of money, though it is accustomed to allow many kinds of money which are different in a genetic sense. The co-existence of many different kinds of money which are genetically different must be considered later. It gives rise to other classifications, which we call *functional*, and which, on account of their totally different basis,[1] must be strictly separated from the genetic classification. A great deal of the confusion in classification of currencies arises from neglect of this distinction.

The classification of means of payment into pensatory and proclamatory is, as we have already seen, genetic; our concept of money is therefore genetic, as it signifies Chartal means of payment.

The concept of specie money, which we have not yet discussed, is also genetic.

---

[1] *Fundamentum divisionis.*—TR.

On the other hand, the concept, for example, of current money, small change and valuta money is entirely functional, as will be seen later. We have not yet anything to do with this classification and only mention it here for the moment in order to dismiss it.

The genetic classification has in the first place the three characteristics already mentioned.

(1) The means of payment are either pensatory or proclamatory.

(2) They are either morphic or amorphic.

(3) They are either hylogenic or autogenic.

The characteristics now appear in the following scheme, on which the genetic classification is based.

Means of payment are			
Pensatory (can only be hylogenic).		Proclamatory (can only be morphic).	
Amorphic.	Morphic.	These means of payment are Chartal. Chartal means of payment = money.	
Autometallism comes here.	The example of the ducats (p. 28) comes here.		
I	II	Hylogenic.	Autogenic.
		III & IV (see below).	V & VI (see below).

I. The first kind is an authylic means of payment,

as in practice only metals are the material; this means autometallistic means of payment.

Bar form is sufficient. The form of coins is not excluded, so long as we mean coin only in the technical sense. But the form of the coins must not have any legal significance.

II. The second kind (morphic-pensatory means of payment) always appears in the form of coins. The metal is immaterial. But it should be noticed that all coins do not come under this head, but only those which are used according to their actual weight.

The form here described is so rare that we had to invent our previous example of the ducats with pensatory use (p. 28).

III–VI. All four are money proper. It should be noticed that there are both hylogenic and autogenic moneys, and also two sub-classes of each, to which we shall return later.

The more exact classification of Chartal means of payment, *i. e.* money, we must defer once again. We must now give an account of the kind of satisfaction which is produced through the use of Chartal means of payment.

§ 3. *Use in Circulation*

The receiver of pensatory payments has the choice between use in the arts and use in circulation.

If he decides for the former or technical use, he considers very closely the nature and quantity of the material. If, however, he decides for the use in circulation he considers only their legal validity as means of payment.

When we consider the want that is satisfied by Chartal means of payment—money—we cannot make the general assertion that the satisfaction is in no case " real," for there are kinds of money which offer " real " satisfaction though belonging to the Chartal system. For example, specie money, a difficult concept which we shall come to know by and by, has the form of a Chartal means of payment and yet has the property, at any rate when not diminished in weight, of giving real satisfaction in the same way as a morphic pensatory means of payment.

A great many other kinds of money, whether coins or warrants, regarded as material, either cannot be used technically at all (paper) or only in a way which would involve great loss, so that in their case real satisfaction is in practice excluded.

Money, then, generally speaking offers no certainty of " real " satisfaction, but an absolutely sure satisfaction through circulation.

The common feature, then, in all means of payment is that the holder uses them in circulation as soon as he is in a position to hand over units of value. The satisfaction, therefore, of the holder does not depend on possession *per se*, but on possession with a view to future use for payment.

Their distinction is that pensatory means of pay-

ment can always be put to technical use, and give
" real " satisfaction, while Chartal means of payment
may or may not do so.

Why is the man in the street always so distrustful
at the absence of the " real " satisfaction ?   Apparently from the following reasons.

A lytric debt can only be reduced or paid off
through the delivery of an object (a pound of copper),
or perhaps also by the delivery of another object
(silver) substituted for it by the State; in any case,
however, only by such objects as, even apart from
legal ordinance, form an economic commodity.

But there are Chartal pieces (*e. g.* warrants and
notes) which, apart from legal ordinance, are not
economic commodities.   What does a scrap of paper
considered *per se* represent ?   Clearly nothing.

The man in the street, reasoning thus, considers it
justifiable to separate the means of payment from
the legal ordinance, to subject them to criticism in
the light of nature and, if their material is no longer
an economic commodity, to reject them.   He is in
the mood to speak of " a scrap of paper," on seeing
before him a Chartal piece in this form, or if he
should be required to take it in payment.

When, however, he himself tenders the piece and the
other man shows signs of using the expression about
a scrap of paper, the tables are turned and he calls
the other an ignoramus.

But it is wrong to judge Chartal pieces turn and

turn about alternately in their legal aspect and in
the light of nature. Payment is a legal proceeding,
and it is sufficient that the Chartal pieces should be
legally valid.

In speaking of debt each man in his native innocence
thinks of himself as the creditor and judges the means
of payment from the standpoint of their acceptability
to himself.

But from my own point of view there are, besides
the debts in which I am a creditor, others in respect
of which I am a debtor. The latter are called first
and foremost my " debts," the others are my claims.

The concept " debt " is *amphibolic;* i. e., if indebtedness is the relation between two people, it is not laid
down which of the two is to be creditor and which
debtor.

For the one, the debt is positive; he is called the
debtor. For the other, it is negative; he is the
creditor. Negative debts are claims.

Therefore the converse is also true, that the concept
of a claim is amphibolic. If a claim exists between
two persons, it is not in the first place laid down
which of the two is creditor and which debtor.

For the one the claim is positive—he is the creditor;
for the other, it is negative—he is the debtor.
Negative claims are debts.

The principle we have so often mentioned, that the
State maintains existing debts, is better stated in
the following way: " The State maintains in each

individual case both negative and positive debts," or, if you like, "The State maintains in each case both negative and positive claims." When the State introduces new means of payment, this takes effect in reference to the negative and positive debts of each person, or—what comes to the same thing—his negative and his positive claims.

Each individual has an *amphitropic* position in trade, *i. e.* he is in some quarters a debtor and at the same time in other quarters a creditor.

This amphitropic position of the individual in economic transactions was so obvious that it was completely overlooked.

The objection of the layman to means of payment like the much-decried inconvertible paper money is always based on his mistake of looking at the position in economic transactions *monotropically ;* he thinks of himself as always creditor.

He makes two mistakes : he regards such Chartal means of payment under their natural, not their legal aspect, and secondly, he considers his own position in trade monotropically, not amphitropically.

If, however, we avoid those two mistakes, it will no longer seem strange that there can also be a money of a material which, apart from the law, is no longer a " commodity."

If the man in the street now raises the practical question that he does not want to have the paper Chartal form at all, it seems to him dangerous, a

menace to the general weal, he may very likely be
right, but he is going outside the domain of theory—
as indeed he likes to do, for the natural man has
the temperament of a public man; he wishes, in
laudable anxiety for the general welfare, to employ
his activities in bringing the Good to birth. And
who would wish to put obstacles in his path?

This, however, is not the attitude of the theorist.
He must follow lytric forms, both good and bad, with
equal attention. He will not begin by giving advice,
but by laying down principles. For him the essence
of a thing is something quite different from its practical
importance. His temperament is not that of the
public man, but of the philosopher.

The system, dangerous in practice, pleases him
because essential characteristics are there most easily
recognisable, but he takes care not to recommend
such a system. He is not there to make recommen-
dations but to explain phenomena. He leaves to the
public man the business of bringing the Good to
birth; and the most influential public man is often
the weakest theorist.

When once money has been stripped of material
content, the reproach is usually made that no " real "
payment in the proper sense of the word can now be
made. Of course not, if by payment is meant payment by something material. But jurisprudence has
to adapt itself to political authority. The law
recognises such payments on occasions, and therefore

E

they are for the jurist true payments, and jurisprudence is forced to broaden correspondingly the
earlier narrow concept of payment.

There is also another objection which is often
raised against non-material Chartal money. Such
tickets as paper money pure and simple are, it is said,
acknowledgments of the State's indebtedness. Payment in such tickets is therefore only a claim on the
State, a provisional satisfaction still leaving something
to be done on the part of the State. It is not a
definitive payment, consequently not a payment at
all in the strict sense. It is alleged in support of
this contention that the Austrian State notes of
1866, which were undoubtedly paper money in the
strictest sense of the word, even bore the inscription
National Debt Office (*die Staats-Schuldenverwaltung*).

Here, however, it must be recalled that the inscription on Chartal pieces is not a source of information
as to the legal nature of the pieces, but is only a
distinguishing mark.

The question is, how these pieces stand in the eye
of the law. On their face they may admit that they
are debts, but in point of fact they are not so if the
debts are not meant to be paid. In the case of paper
money proper the State offers no other means of
payment; therefore it is not an acknowledgment of
the State's indebtedness, even if this is expressly
stated. The statement is only a political good
intention, and it is not actually true that the State
will convert it into some other means of payment.

The decisive factor is not what the State would do if it could, but what the State does. It is therefore a complete mistake to see no actual payment in payment by inconvertible paper money. It is a true payment, though it is not material.

If it is said that the State makes the greatest efforts to give up that paper system and to convert its notes into material money as soon as it can, and that the notes accordingly are a claim on it for better money to come later, and therefore a debt of the State, what are we to say in reply?

The answer is that the notes are still not a debt of the State in the legal sense, but at most appear to be so in the course of legal history when the State shows the intention of altering the means of payment some time or other, and of changing the present means of payment, according to some proportion to be found later, into new means of payment.

To judge by that intention, the notes can be called a debt of the State; but in this sense any means of payment, even the autometallistic ones, are a debt of the State. On this account, therefore, the title of true definitive means of payment should not be refused to the notes.

This is not difficult to see. Every new means of payment is named by its units of value; and every new unit is stated in terms of the former one.

The old becomes a claim on the new one at the moment of the introduction of the new, for as the

State does not extinguish existing debts, so it does not extinguish existing means of payment.

The fact that the State might like to give up inconvertible paper money for " better " means of payment is therefore no ground for thinking of paper money as a debt of the State in some sense different from that of " more solid " means of payment.

In the course of ages all means of payment are subject to change. A note would only be a debt in the legal sense if it were convertible without any radical general change in the means of payment, and this the note according to our premises certainly is not.

Instead of perpetually insisting on the defects of autogenic money, just think a little of its services. It frees us from our debts, and a man who gets rid of his debts does not need to spend time considering whether his means of payment were material or not. First and foremost it frees us from our debts towards the State, for the State, when emitting it, acknowledges that, in receiving, it will accept this means of payment. The greater the part played by the taxes, the more important is this fact to the tax-payer.

Payment with non-material money (I do not say with immaterial money) is for the country of its origin just as genuine a payment as any other. It is sufficient for the needs of domestic trade; in fact it makes such trade possible. It does not indeed satisfy certain other demands, but the phenomenon is not in itself abnormal.

Phenomena are only abnormal in so far as they conflict with our cherished preconceptions. Non-material Chartal money is not constructed according to the requirements of the schools. It is not narrow school tradition but actual fact which should teach us the essential principles of Chartal payment.

The non-material Chartal form is not abnormal. On the contrary, it gives the bare normal lay-figure to be draped in all manner of imposing and useful fashions.

A parallel case is the constitution of an army. It may be highly expedient to equip an army with breechloaders, because it will then be a better match for the enemy. But this technical circumstance is not the essence of an army, which is an administrative whole whether well equipped or the reverse. So it is with the monetary system. It is an administrative phenomenon, which must be conceived as such, before preference is given to this or that means of payment.

No theory of the metallists deals fairly with non-material money. The theory of the chartalists which we have here explained has room both for material and for non-material money. It is perfectly harmless, as it recommends nothing, and perfectly adequate, as it explains everything.

One thing indeed the chartalist admits without more ado. In the case of non-material Chartal money, as we have described it hitherto, the unit of value is not defined " really," *i. e.* in material. We cannot say a pound of copper, an ounce of silver or so many grammes of gold compose the unit of value. This does not mean that the unit of value is not defined at all, but that it is defined historically. This is the perfectly clear logical consequence of the fact that law contents itself with defining and naming the means of payment and relating them back to an earlier unit. The law never says that the means of payment are such and such a quantity of material, but merely gives them a name and description.

As soon as the State has advanced to the Chartal means of payment, the mutual relations of the concepts are changed.

In former times the unit of value was defined " really," *i. e.* in terms of material. Debts in units of value arose from this, and the means of payment were the result of the definition of the unit of value (*e. g.* it was copper, if the pound of copper was the unit of value).

On the introduction of the Chartal form, however, the situation is as follows. Debts exist expressed in the earlier unit of value. The present unit of value is not defined " really," but by the declaration by the State how many of the present units (say marks) go to discharge the debt expressed in the former unit (say thaler). To know the means of payment we need, not a mere historical definition, but a special description of the pieces, and a statement how many units of value each piece is worth. The resulting validity is purely authoritative; a definite content for the pieces is neither demanded nor excluded.

In former times the unit of value had to be "really" defined, *i. e.* in some material. Hence arose debts in units of value. Now we know of debts in earlier units of value, and by reason of these debts the present unit is defined no longer "really" but historically.

No conclusion can be drawn about the means of payment from the definition of the unit of value because this definition has ceased to be a "real one."

All this holds good in every Chartal system, therefore in every kind of money, even in the most popular kind, namely, specie money, as we shall soon show.

This is perhaps the boldest assertion that can be ventured, for nothing is so directly opposed to the common view. People will retort that these propositions may be true in the case of paper money, but in the case of specie money they are false. Nevertheless, the great dividing wall between the means of payment is not between hard cash and paper, but between pensatory and Chartal means of payment.

Specie money has all the properties of paper money and a few others in addition.

§ 4. *The Platic and Genetic Relations of Money to the Metals*

The relations of money to the metals are most easily classified into platic, genetic and dromic.

We have platic relations when we confine our consideration of the finished pieces to their nature as " pieces " or discs.[1]

Genetic relations appear as soon as we inquire whether a certain kind of money can only be created through the use of a certain metal conceived by the law as destined at all times for conversion into money. Certain kinds of money arise thus, others in other ways.

Dromic relations appear when the question is asked whether a metal has a fixed price secured to it or not.

The definition of specie money [2] will emerge from the consideration of genetic relations, which are by far the most important.

The least important division is the platic, which is precisely the one nearest to the heart of the man in the street. Technically we find coins on the one side, warrants [3] or notes on the other.

Coins are stamped discs made of metal. Warrants are stamped discs of paper, leather or silk or any other non-metallic material. Coins, again, are of precious metals and of base metals. Precious metals are those which do not oxidise easily, especially gold and silver.

---

[1] *Platten.*   [2] *Bares Geld*, hard cash.   [3] *Scheine.*

Coined money always has a certain Mint standard. If a certain coin, *e. g.* a sovereign, is to be made, such and such a metal is to be used, and out of a given weight of this metal so many pieces of equal weight are to be coined.

The Mint standard then does not say whether this or that metal is to be freely converted into money, but, assuming that this or that coin is to be produced, it lays down technical rules for the production. The Mint standard lays down what metal is to be used and what is to be the content of the equal pieces. In the case of precious metals it is the custom in Germany to name only the fine content and not the alloy, which, however, is also prescribed.

Just as the Mint standard says nothing as to the free or conditional conversion of a metal into money, so it also says nothing as to the validity of each piece. Fixing the validity of the pieces is a special act of law. This is the essence of chartality.

The consequence is accordingly that, for each kind of coined money, the validity must be expressly and separately stated.

This is most clearly evident if a coin has a proper name, *e. g.* the English sovereign. The prescription that 40 lb. troy standard gold go to make 1869 sovereigns gives the Mint standard, but in this nothing is said as to the validity of these coins. The proposition that the sovereign is worth £1 sterling is a separate proposition which is added to the definition of the

Mint standard. The settlement of the validity of
the coin is not part of the Mint technique, but of
Chartal law. This circumstance is easily overlooked
by the metallists, who never can get rid of the idea
that the unit of value is represented by a given
quantity of metal.

So, that ordinance which states the Mint standard
of the sovereign does not yet add the further proposition that all gold is convertible into sovereigns
without limit.

A similar example in Germany would be this—
the Mint standard of our gold coin (since 1871) called
krone requires that, when there is a coining at all,
$139\frac{1}{2}$ pieces be coined from a pound of fine gold.

It is not required that the gold be coined without
limit nor settled how many marks the krone is worth.
The settlement of the validity is effected by the special
prescription laying down, *e. g.* that the sovereign is
worth £1 sterling, the German krone worth ten marks,
" the German copper pfennig $\frac{1}{100}$th part of a mark,"
the specific content of a krone $\frac{1}{1395}$th part of a pound
of fine gold, because that quantity of gold is contained
in every piece of this validity. The specific content
of the silver German mark is $\frac{1}{100}$th of a pound of
fine silver, because every piece of that validity has
that amount of silver in it—we mean, of course, at the
moment when it is coined. The German thaler has
the specific content of $\frac{1}{90}$th part of a pound of fine
silver, because every piece of a thaler's validity

contains that amount of fine silver. Notice that the
thaler and the two-mark piece do not have the same
specific content, for the settlement of the validity is
not bound up with the content.

The same result as from specific content can be
obtained from " specific " validity, which gives their
reciprocal relations, *e. g.* from a pound troy of standard
gold there are coined $\frac{1869}{40}$ pounds sterling in
sovereigns; out of the bullion which contains a pound
of fine gold, 1395 marks are coined in kronen.

If the specific validity is stated, or its reciprocal
expression, the specific content, the old-fashioned
mint terminology used the words " to bring out "
(*ausbringen*); the pound of fine silver was brought
out into thirty thalers (unit of value), as now brought
out into 100 two-mark pieces.

So long as we do not depart from the platic subdivision, it is quite impossible to discover specie
money. Many people think that coins of precious
metal are specie money. Sometimes this is so, but
there are coins of precious metal which are not specie
money, *e. g.* thalers after 1871.

On the other hand, in ancient times there were
coins of copper, a base metal, which were certainly
to be counted as specie money.

The platic classification is not very fruitful. The
valuable knowledge of the Master of the Mint and
the enviable erudition of our Numismatists are to be
held in honour, but neither the one nor the other

brings us much farther than a knowledge of the contents and impressions of the coins, and both seem unable to contribute to our knowledge of the real nature of the means of payment.

Lytrology cannot be built on a basis of numismatics in spite of the fact that the oldest means of payment, as soon as they are money, make their appearance as coins. But the genetic classification of kinds of money goes to the root of the matter. Let us fix our attention on the conditions laid down by law for the conversion of metal into money.

In the times of autometallism the law chooses a certain metal to be the means of exchange; in the early days of chartality people still clung to the notion of a particular metal being physically convertible into money pieces in unlimited quantities. Every such metal we will call hylic. It is no longer *per se* a means of exchange, but it is thought necessary to the existence of money, which as a general rule comes about through coining.

Money, then, is still hylogenic and thereby connected with autometallism.

The difference is that pensatory bars or pensatory coins are paid out by weight, but money is not; the resemblance, that in both cases the quantity of the hylic metal fixes the amount of the means of payment.

Without hylic metal no means of payment—that is the principle which is carried over from autometallism into the Chartal system, but only with reference to hylogenic money. Hyle [1] now signifies a metal (we need not consider other materials) which in accordance with the system may be converted into money without limit. If there is a limit the metal ceases to be hylic, so that, for instance, in Germany, copper, nickel and silver are not hylic; gold, on the contrary, is.

Gold is hylic not from its use in the arts, but from the legal regulation which, as it were, confers on it a patent of nobility, allowing money to be made from it without limit.

Now, however, the question arises : Given the hylic metal, how many units of value in money can be made from one unit of weight of this metal ? The answer is given by a special regulation, which we will call the hylogenic norm.

Given the hylic metal and the unit of value, the norm lays it down that each unit of value in money is to be made of so many units of weight of the hylic metal, *e. g.* a £1 sterling is to be made from every $\frac{40}{1869}$ parts of a pound troy of standard gold.

Given the hylic metal and the unit of weight, the norm lays it down that so many units of value in money are to be made therefrom, *e. g.* from a pound troy of standard gold $\frac{1869}{40}$ths of a pound sterling. Either formula will do.

The norm is a concept which escapes the metallists; for the chartalists, it is the key to the understanding of hylogenic money.

In the case of autogenic money, the concept of the norm does not exist, because there is in this case no hylic metal, even if the discs of the autogenic money are made of metal.

The norm has nothing to do with the Mint standard, for the question is not one of coins. It is only laid down that the hylic metal can be converted without limit into money, and that by the prescribed validity one unit of weight shall give rise to a given number of units of value in money.

When in Germany before 1871 silver was a hylic metal, the norm said that from one pound of silver, money to the amount of thirty thalers was to be made.

Now that gold is the hylic metal, the norm says that, from one pound of gold, money to the amount of 1395 marks is to be made. In both cases the production was unlimited; this is essential to the concept of a hylic metal.

Specie money, the commonest and most important case of hylogenic money, implies the existence of a hylic metal and its norm, and its norm too for a definite time. This imports a time condition into the concept that we are seeking. If, then, such a metal is converted into money by coining, and if the coined pieces have such a validity that their specific content corresponds to the hylic norm, in this case these pieces are specie money.

Therefore the State has three rules to lay down :

(1) Coins (minutely described) are made from a given metal with a given absolute content. This is the Mint standard.

(2) Each of these coins must be worth so many units of value. The unit of value is either that previously existing or it is newly specified, and in this case it is historically defined with reference to the previous unit of value. This gives the absolute validity. The specific content follows immediately from the regulations, as also its reciprocal expression, the specific validity. It remains, however, undecided whether the coins are money or not.

(3) Finally, it is laid down whether the metal named is to be converted into money with or without limit. If with a limit, those coins are not specie money. If without a limit, the number of units of value into which the limit of weight of metal is to be converted is prescribed.

This is the hylogenic norm; and those coins are specie money in which the specific content answers to that norm.

Coins can, however, still be recognised as money if they were specie money according to an earlier norm, and their specific content is not less than that laid down by the new norm.

It is easily seen that in the definition of specie money it is not the Mint standard that matters, but that the specific content of the piece should have the aforesaid relation to the hylogenic norm.

All attempts to define specie money by the Mint standard alone are perfectly hopeless, except for those persons who regard the content of the piece as the source of its validity—that is, for the metallists. They have the advantage of defining specie money more simply, but they cannot conceive autogenic money, and therefore cannot define it. They have no universally applicable concept of money.

The chartalist, seeking just such a conception, can give to specie money no such simple definition; but from his own definition he infers that since 1871 thalers are no longer specie money, for silver is no longer a hylic metal and for the same reason the silver coins of the German Empire (five marks, two marks, one mark, half a mark) are not specie money. Neither are the copper and nickel coins specie money, for copper and nickel are not hylic metals.

Before 1871 the thalers were specie money, because silver was a hylic metal and the specific content of the thalers corresponded to the hylogenic norm; the silver groschen was not specie money, for, although it was a silver coin, its specific content was less than that of a thaler.

In South Germany, prior to 1871, gulden pieces were specie money. Besides them there were also in circulation crown thalers, a silver coin from the Austrian Lowlands which was no longer coined. Were crown thalers specie money?

Yes, for it does not matter whether the thalers were

still coined or not, but whether the silver was hylic, that is, convertible into money without limit. Also the specific content of the crown thaler corresponded to the norm for converting the silver into money. The crown thaler had the same specific content as the gulden, its specific content therefore coincided with the norm at that time. The crown thalers, therefore, were then specie money.

In Northern Germany in the year 1871 there were two kinds of thalers, the older kind coined before 1857 and the newer coined after that date.

The older ones had a somewhat higher specific content, as fourteen pieces were coined from the mark fine—the then unit of weight—and this did not completely coincide with the specific content of the newer thalers—thirty pieces from the pound fine.

For Chartal theory this somewhat involved case is easily explained, while the metallistic theory is completely bewildered, for how can a heavy thaler be worth just the same as a light? For us, however, the notion of validity is independent of the content. The metal remains hylic even when the norm changes. In the centuries when silver was a hylic metal in England, the norm underwent continual alteration until the time of Queen Elizabeth—more and more pence were produced from the unit of weight of the hylic metal. As long as the alteration continued in the direction of making the new pennies of the same denomination continually lighter, the pennies of the

F

older currency did not cease to be specie money (though the astute merchant did not use them for payment), for they still fulfil the condition of the definition, *i. e.* their specific content still answers to the norm, inasmuch as it is not smaller than the later norm.

Now if in the course of history the norm alters in the opposite sense, if the specific content of the older pieces is less than that laid down by the later norm, they then cease to be specie money, while yet remaining money and continuing to have the same validity.

In modern times changes of the norm are less frequent in case of the same hylic metal, and the definition of specie money is therefore simpler for the newer developments of currency than for the older.

An international name for specie money is very desirable. We will call it *orthotypic* in order to indicate that the specific content of the pieces is dependent on that norm ("ortho-"). So non-specie kinds of money might be called " notal " or *paratypic* money, to show that it is counter to (para) that norm.

Attempts have been made before to formulate the difference between orthotypic and paratypic money, but specie money presupposes the concepts of chartality and hylic metal, and both concepts are new. Hence also paratypic money could not be defined.

Credit money has sometimes been contrasted with specie money, from the mistaken idea that paratypic money was properly speaking convertible into specie money, which is not invariably the case.

It would be just as wrong to hold that paratypic money can never give " real " satisfaction. The discs may or may not be made of worthless material. If, for example, while silver still remained non-hylic, the price of silver in London again went as high as in 1871, our thalers, while paratypic, would still give a " real " satisfaction, only the " real " satisfaction would not be hylic.

The root idea of specie money is that it shall be a Chartal means of payment but have a hylic minimum content. This is obviously half-way house between a clearly conscious autohylism and a dimly felt chartality. The hylic content is the pledge which the holder keeps (1) against the disappearance of chartality if the State and its law should perish; (2) more seriously in order to have money to use outside the country in foreign trade.

As to hylic money, we have not required that only one metal should be recognised by the State as hylic; more than one metal can have this position, *e. g.* gold and silver, as in the case of bimetallism; and there can be different kinds of specie money, *e. g.* specie gold money as well as specie silver money.

Almost everyone holds that the definition of the unit of value is contained in the hylogenic norm; this is the essence of the metallistic theory, and, accordingly, the German unit of value or mark would be defined as the $\frac{1}{1395}$th part of a pound of fine gold.

What happens then if, as in France after 1803, two metals are admitted as hylic, and therefore there are two hylogenic norms? Which of these gives the definition of the unit of value? Is the franc the $\frac{1}{200}$th part of a kilogramme of Mint silver $\frac{9}{10}$ths fine, or the $\frac{1}{3100}$th part of a kilogramme of Mint gold $\frac{9}{10}$ths fine? The monometallist answers, this is just why bimetallism is illogical; either one or the other definition must be recognised.

The bimetallist rejoins that the two definitions are alternative : sometimes the one applies, sometimes the other; there is therefore no logical contradiction.

Neither disputant is right, for the hylogenic norm is not the definition of the unit of value; there can be currencies without a hylic metal and therefore without a hylogenic norm, but never currencies without a unit of value.

The legislator himself may think that he is defining the unit of value when he lays down the hylogenic norm; but he only has the decisive word when he is laying down his law; when it comes to the giving of definitions, the legislator's power ceases and that of the theorist begins. The unit of value is, as we know, historically defined, and has nothing to do with the hylogenic norm, for it precedes the norm.

As hylogenic money has a sub-class in specie money, so autogenic money has a sub-class, of great practical importance, called—very vaguely—pure and simple paper money, which is as universally contemned as specie money is universally esteemed.

As the warrants in our platic classification usually consist of paper, paper money in the proper sense of the term comes under the heading warrants, but this is hardly a good definition, for there are warrants that are not paper money pure and simple, and this last cannot be defined platically, but only genetically, like specie money.

Money is autogenic when it is not made by the conversion of a hylic metal into money; and it has no norm, gaining its validity by proclamation without the requirement of a hylic metal.

This, however, does not exclude the use of metal discs, as we have seen above when we spoke of the old silver groschen. They are coins, even silver coins, and yet they are classed among autogenic moneys.

The form of a coin is therefore possible for autogenic money; but it is also permissible in the form of notes, and this brings us to " proper " paper money. It is *papyroplatic* autogenic money.

We are not speaking here of convertibility or inconvertibility, but dealing only with the origin, which is non-hylic, and with the paper material of the notes. Where both these are united we have pure and simple paper money in the genetic sense, a fact which is clearly brought out in the systematic name " autogenic paper money."

In this case, therefore, no hylic metal is used as the basis for the money, neither for coining, nor as a reserve kept by the State creating the money.

By far the most important kinds of money are specie money and autogenic paper money.

Money must be first classified into hylogenic and autogenic. Then hylogenic money is classified into orthotypic and the reverse; then autogenic into metalloplatic and papyroplatic.

The connection is shown below in the form of a diagram.

Money is			
Hylogenic.		Autogenic.	
Orthotypic.	Not orthotypic.	Metalloplatic.	Not metalloplatic.
(1) Specie money, orthotypic money.	(2)	(3)	(4) Autogenic paper money.

On account of the importance of the contrast between specie money (1) and the other sorts of money, we include (2) (3) and (4) under the expression "paratypic." Paratypic sorts of money have no uniform content. All that they have in common is that none of them is specie money.

Hylogenic paratypic money (2) in the above table comes about when hylic metal must be handed over

to the State making the money. The State then
issues pieces for it in accordance with the norm,
not in the way, however, of orthotypic coining, but,
e. g. through the issue of warrants. If in Germany
every pound of gold handed over was paid for with
1395 marks in warrants (*Kassenscheine*),[1] these
would not be hylogenic but paratypic, and also
papyroplatic. Considered technically, they could not
be distinguished from paper money, but genetically the
difference from autogenic paper money is quite evident, for they would be hylogenic paper money, which
would not be exposed to the same disfavour as the
other.

But the papyroplatic variety is only mentioned as
an example. It might also happen that every pound
handed in might be paid for in 1395 marks as before,
but that this sum might be paid in thalers. In this
case the thalers would be hylogenic, indeed *chrysogenic*
money, but they would be *argyroplatic,* and therefore
not orthotypic, for gold has remained our hylic metal,
while the thalers are made of silver. Such a form is
incomprehensible from the point of view of the metallist, while it offers not the smallest difficulty to the
chartalist. In Holland, though this system is not laid
down in actual ordinances, the Dutch silver gulden
is a near approach to chrysogenic argyroplatic money.

This brings out very clearly the difference between
the platic and the genetic point of view, for anyone

---

[1] Pay-office warrants or certificates.

considering the discs would never discover the connection of the money with the hylic metal gold.

Autogenic metalloplatic money (3) is widely used. In Germany since 1871 it embraces first the thalers, then all silver pieces coined by the Empire, thirdly, all nickel and copper coins.

We shall discuss later the fact that the thalers are (1905) *current* money and the other coins we have named are small change. What is important is not their difference, but what they have in common—the fact that they are not now of hylic origin, although they all occur in the form of coins. This is the reason why many writers—for example, even Bamberger—are inclined to call the thalers a kind of small change, a terminological awkwardness arising from a right feeling, a premonition of the autogenic nature of these kinds of coins.

Even in the earlier German monetary system (before 1871) copper money was in this position, and also the silver groschen which we have already discussed (p. 64).

It is very remarkable that in spite of its wide diffusion and early origin, autogenic metalloplatic money was never correctly classified in the monetary system, for the concept of hylic metal had not been developed.

If we refer back to p. 43 it is easy to give a general genetic classification of means of payment in which there are six divisions in all, *i. e.* besides the four

kinds of money, two kinds of means of payment
which are not money (see diagram below).

Means of payment are					
Pensatory.		Chartal, *i. e.* money.			
Amorphic.	Morphic.	Hylogenic.		Autogenic.	
		Ortho-typic.	Not ortho-typic.	Metallo-platic.	Not metallo-platic.
I.	II.	(1) III.	(2) IV.	(3) V.	(4) VI.

I, II, III and IV are hylogenic, V and VI are
autogenic.

I is amorphic.   II, III, IV, V and VI are morphic.

II is usually metalloplatic, and III and V invariably
so.   In the case of I the platic nature is not requisite,
and therefore not the metalloplatic.

VI is not metalloplatic, because this is required by
the basis of classification.

In the case of IV the question whether it is metalloplatic or not is left undecided, in order to avoid a
further subdivision; both forms are possible.

It should be noted that metalloplatic is a wider
concept than *hyloplatic.*

This classification is not pragmatic, *i. e.* does not
give the rules of any particular country nor lay
down what metal is hylic at any particular time.

It very often happens that the State is itself

uncertain as to the nature of the means of payment and makes inconsistent ordinances. Traces of a relapse into the pensatory system can be found long after the Chartal system is in force.

Among these are the regulations as to least current weight. In the German Empire, least current weight has been abolished in the case of all paratypic coins. However diminished in weight, the thalers are always worth three marks, as long as they are at all recognisable; and so with the silver, copper and nickel coins of the German Empire. This is absolutely right under the Chartal system of currency, where validity is independent of content. On the other hand, for orthotypic money (gold coins) least current weight is retained. If the loss of weight in these pieces is more than $\frac{1}{2}$ per cent., they are no longer valid in private circulation.

The least current weight is therefore $99\frac{1}{2}$ per cent. of the prescribed weight. This is a quite unnecessary relapse into the pensatory system. If the Chartal system is intended to abolish weighing, what is the meaning of this regulation, which again calls in the scales?

Obviously it is to assure to the private person in any case a " real " satisfaction, if only to that small extent. The rule, however, is completely superfluous, for, quite rightly, in Germany the State remains bound to take even the most worn pieces as if of full weight *i. e.* according to their validity by proclamation.

No doubt it serves to prevent the orthotypic money in circulation from being worn quite away, and to keep the pieces easily recognisable, and it is also important with regard to the *dromic* arrangements to be considered later.

All this, however, can be easily attained without the rule of least current weight for the private person, which only interferes with the unhesitating acceptance of the pieces.

Many States, *e. g.* France, have long ago abolished it, even in the case of orthotypic money.

We do not mean to recommend that wearing down should be allowed to go on without let or hindrance, as in ancient times, when the pieces were only reminted when their thinness had become quite unbearable. This is gross negligence; but does not justify least current weight for the private person.

Suppose a sudden reminting takes place because the pieces have worn very thin; the old coins must be called in and replaced by new ones. In this case the State can either take old coins by weight or take them according to their validity by proclamation. The first is more profitable for the State from the fiscal point of view, for the loss of weight falls on the holder, whoever he may be. The other method entails a sacrifice for the State, divided among the tax-payers.

The question who bears the burden is worth consideration, but it belongs rather to the domain of financial policy. From the lytrological point of view another question arises : What is the governing principle ? If the State redeems by weight, it is treating money as pensatory. If, however, it redeems the money in accordance with its validity by proclamation, then its action is consistent, for it is not permissible to consider money first in one light and then in another in accordance with the balance of advantage and disadvantage.

If the principles had always been kept perfectly distinct, there could never have been a pensatory redemption of money. Opinions, however, were confused and the State sometimes inclined to the one, sometimes to the other view, in each case to the one which appeared the more profitable, wavering between the metallistic and the chartalistic point of view. Even kings were metallists when they took money, and chartalists when they issued it.

Another uncertainty was prevalent before 1871 in South Germany. From the fact that silver was a hylic metal, people drew the conclusion that foreign silver coins were straightway to be admitted as money. All that was necessary was to arrange the validity so that the specific content of the pieces was in agreement with the hylic norm. Thus, awkwardly, the validity came about by custom and the State gave its blessing retrospectively. This proceeding, of course, is not inconsistent with the Chartal theory, for the foreign coins, once recognised, are validated by proclamation and the foreign stamp is no obstacle in. itself if the law has given its approval. But the State loses all power to make its money easily recognisable, and the varied complexity of kinds of money baffles supervision and control.

It followed, of course, from the hylogenic norm that foreign silver coins were convertible into native silver money, but not necessarily by an offhand validation of the pieces.

That proceeding would be comparatively bearable if foreign coins were only recognised after they had lost their property of being money abroad. If, however, they are still currency abroad, the pieces acquire the peculiar double position which we recognise under the name of *synchartism ;* they are subject to two legal systems—that of the State which produces them, on the one hand, and that of the State which recognises them, on the other. The arrangement is sometimes intentional; but if it happens through indifference—not to say thoughtlessness—it is objectionable, for the State thereby loses a part of its control over its currency.

The highest pitch of folly was reached in South Germany after 1871, after silver had lost its hylic position. At that time the Austrian silver gulden was allowed in circulation as a two-mark piece, and it was a source of rejoicing that it contained more silver than the silver coins of the Empire. Here the fact was overlooked that the earlier admission of foreign

silver coins was at any rate based on the hylic
property of the silver, the reminting of which was
foolishly neglected.

After 1871, however, this reason could no longer
be alleged; and yet from old habit the silver coins
were admitted into circulation in South Germany as
two-mark pieces, while the laws of the Empire laid
an absolute ban on the free coinage of silver two-mark
pieces. Had this abuse been suffered longer, the
Empire would have lost all control over its paratypic
silver money, while its first principle is to retain this
control. The German public continued to live com-
fortably in the belief that silver was still hylic.

It is quite absurd in such a complicated business as
our currency to work with customary law; the time
for that is long past. The penetration of the Austrian
silver gulden, after the year 1871, in South Germany,
was its last (short-lived) success. Since that time this
source of legal inconsistency has fortunately been
cut off.

§ 5. *Dromic Relations of Money to Metal*

The control of currency—in more general terms
lytric control—has sometimes the aim of giving a
fixed price to a certain metal, and this it achieves by
special measures which we will call hylodromic. All
acts of this control, so far as they are directed to
that end, we will call hylodromy for short. (i) Only
hylic metal can be made amenable to such price

regulation. This explains the first part of the new word.

(ii) As to the second part, certain prices are called usually " current " prices; so as to make a more convenient adjective we use the Greek word " dromos," an arbitrary but permissible proceeding; *hylodromy*, therefore, means for us the deliberate fixing of the price of a hylic metal, or, still more accurately, the deliberate delimitation, both upwards and downwards, of the price of a hylic metal. We must now describe this particular kind of lytric control in detail.

There is one form of the means of payment in which the goal is attained automatically, *ex definitione*, i. e. as a result of the concept of the system. This is the amorphic pensatory means of payment, which we call authylic, or more particularly autometallistic (I, in the table on p. 43).

If a metal is declared hylic and is used as a means of payment by weight, no form being prescribed, there can be no fluctuating price for this metal. It goes without saying that equal weights of this metal can be exchanged for one another. If the pound is the unit of weight, every other pound of that metal also costs a pound, and has therefore a fixed price. This needs no administrative intervention. Hylodromy is already implied in the concept.

In all other lytric forms, however, this has ceased to be the case—a fact so frequently overlooked that it needs special consideration.

Let us suppose that the form is morphic pensatory (II, in table on p. 43). The pieces have then a prescribed form and occur as coins, but they are paid out by weight.

The hylic metal has then an upper limit of price.

No one pays more, for example, for a pound of silver than just a pound of silver; he has that in his hands as a means of payment, or else he cannot think of buying. But the hylic metal has as yet no other price limit. It might quite possibly be cheaper in the form of a bar than a pound of the shaped means of payment (which we postulate), in spite of the identity of the material, *e. g.* if a quantity of unshaped metal were suddenly thrown on the market. The condition that the means of payment must be shaped or formed gives it a distinctive characteristic from the economic point of view.

As a gold goblet is something different from a lump of gold of equal weight, so a gold coin is also something different from the equivalent lump of gold.

If the hylic metal is to have a lower limit of price, one measure is necessary and sufficient; the lytric administration must declare that all bullion appearing in the market can straightway be turned into the prescribed form of coins. The Mint must receive for coinage all metal brought to it. We call this measure *hylolepsy*.

This is not involved in the very notion of a hylic

metal. A metal is hylic when it is convertible into means of payment without limit. This is permission, not compulsion. Hylolepsy implies compulsion.

Hylolepsy is the regulation which must be added so that our hylic metal (in the system of currency we are here discussing) should have a lower limit of price.

Neither of the above two forms of means of payment is as yet money.

Passing to forms of money, and taking first the specie form of money, we find the hylic metal has neither an upper nor a lower limit of price.

The hylic metal has no lower limit of price, for metal brought to market as bullion might easily be sold cheaper than the hylic norm. But in this instance also a hylic metal only means one which may be turned without limit into specie money—a permission, while compulsion is here specially required.

In order to get the lower limit, we must here have the compulsion we call hylolepsy, which is nothing else than what is usually called "free coinage."

The compulsion falls on the lytric administration, and "free" means that the owner of the metal is entitled to offer any quantity he likes for coinage. On the introduction of hylolepsy, the hylic metal has at any rate a lower limit of price, because the lytric administration is compelled to take it in accordance with the lytric norm. In dealing with

G

such a buyer the owner of the bullion does not need to take a lower price.

This is the well-known reason why in Germany gold cannot fall below 1392 marks to the pound, for at that price it is accepted by the lytric administration.

On the other side, however, the hylic metal in a specie form of money has no automatic upper limit.

For it is no part of the system as such that the pieces should always be of full weight. They are constantly losing weight from wearing down, while they yet remain specie money and keep their validity. Full weight is no part of the definition of specie money.

If the hylic metal is to acquire an upper limit of price, we must first make it a special requirement that the pieces of specie money should always be kept up to full weight by withdrawal of light pieces. The fulfilment of this condition first gives the hylic metal the property of having an upper as well as a lower limit.

In Germany gold pieces are withdrawn from circulation as soon as they have lost more than $\frac{1}{2}$ per cent. of the prescribed weight. This fixes an upper limit of price for our hylic metal, for it is now certain that a man holding a minimum of 1395 marks and a maximum of 1400 marks has actually a pound of fine gold.

Least current weight, therefore, in specie money is a special kind of provision that the owner of from

1395 to 1400 marks should possess a pound of fine gold, for the lytric administration secures it for him and makes it evident. We will therefore give this regulation the general name of *hylophantism*, for the word means "placing hylic metal on show." This does not happen directly through the least current weight; but when the least current weight of specie money exists it helps towards hylophantism. Hylophantism is the counterpart of hylolepsy.

Both measures taken together (hylolepsy and hylophantism) produce fixed price limits for the hylic metal, and in the case of specie money are specially necessary, for otherwise, in spite of the specie form, the hylic metal has no fixed price limits.

The hylodromic action of the lytric administration is therefore a combination of the two measures, hylolepsy and hylophantism.

What we have just said of specie money applies not only to the type of money which we have called in our table (p. 70) hylogenic orthotypic, but to hylogenic paratypic money (*i. e.* IV means of payment, (2) kind of money). Hylodromy is confined not to the specie form of money, but to the hylogenic form, a wider concept.

Suppose that an arrangement has been found whereby hylic metal is converted into money in accordance with a norm, but not through coining, so that the State keeps metal and issues notes for it (see above, p. 71). Then the currency is still hylogenic but is now paratypic. If the lytric metal is to have a fixed price, it must be laid down (1) that all hylic metal offered must be turned into money, in this way. This is a hylolepsy, where the lytric administration is bound not indeed to coin, but to "redeem." The effect is the same.

It must be laid down (2) that for every amount of notes handed to the lytric administration, units of weight of hylic metal in accordance with the norm must be given in exchange. This is hylophantism, but the payment may be in bars instead of in coin.[1] Hylodromy can exist without the specie form of money, even without any coining of hylic metal.

At the same time the price of the hylic metal would be fixed, since the upper and lower limits of price would exactly coincide.

We can accordingly distinguish three norms :

(1) The *hylogenic norm* lays it down that hylogenic money shall be made through conversion of a unit of weight of metal into so many units of value (*e. g.* 1395 marks).

(2) The *hyloleptic norm* lays it down that every unit of weight of hylic metal which is offered shall be converted into so many units of value (*e. g.* 1392 marks).

(3) The *hylophantic norm* lays it down that for so many units of value (*e. g.* 1395–1400 marks) a unit of weight of the hylic metal shall be obtainable.

---

[1] As under a Gold Exchange Standard.—TR.

The three norms may or may not coincide. If they coincide, that is hylodromy at its strictest.

If they do not, there are, not fixed prices, but only fixed limits for the price of the hylic metal—a hylodromic range, under a hylogenic monetary system.

We can go no further; as soon as we get monetary systems without hylic metal, hylodromy naturally ceases to exist, for hylodromy implies that a given metal can be converted into money in accordance with a definite norm. If we imagine the hylic metal away, monetary system does not cease, but only the possibility of hylodromy; all metals would be alike to the lytric administration, silver and gold would be what tin and lead now are.

The possibility of a monetary system without a hylic metal (an autogenic system) is easily overlooked, as it is very rare; but it actually exists. There is, as we already know, autogenic paper money; and though there is nearly always specie money (therefore hylogenic money) as well, the specie money, too, can be imagined absent, as will appear when we come to speak of the functional relations of the different kinds of State money.

But we need not think only of paper money. Let us suppose, for example, that before 1871 in Bremen, where foreign gold coins were in constant use as money, there was no legal convertibility of the metal gold into those coins; gold would then not be a hylic metal, and in spite of the platic use of gold, there would have been no hylodromy. For the hyloleptic branch of the lytric administration was missing, even though the hylophantic branch was nearly complete, in the rules limiting the abrasion allowed in those foreign gold coins.

The metal gold would then have had no lower limit of price. In Bremen the gold would not have had a lower, but only an upper price limit.

This phenomenon, which is in any case rare, cannot be made intelligible at all when considered purely from the platic point of view. As a matter of fact the Bremen gold money was not specie money, because there was no hylic metal, in spite of the existence of metal discs.

Really strict hylodromy exists nowhere in practice, but only a delimitation of the hylodromic range. Now this shows the thoughtful observer that hylodromy is not so indispensable as many think. Indeed hylodromy, even the hylodromic range, is very modern.

Hylodromy has been as little the result of conscious invention as chartality, but has simply crept in. When morphic means of payment were invented, no one could foresee how far their underlying principle would depart from pensatory usage; and, with hylogenic money, it was also not obvious how great was the difference in principle from hylodromy, which was at first thoughtlessly assumed to be given with it. For it was always held in former times that autometallism (which is grasped without difficulty) lived on in spite of the addition of the shaping and the validity by proclamation. No one dreamt that these additions had altered the whole basis of the lytric constitution.

Hylolepsy was first applied to orthotypic money because from purely fiscal reasons kings liked to make a profit from seignorage. It was therefore desirable that all hylic metals should be coined, because the hyloleptic deduction accrued to the king's chest. That is the only reason for the rule that all hylic metal must be accepted for coinage. It is quite true that in this way, quite unintentionally, a lower limit of price was created. In legal history arrangements made for one purpose often produce another, and then that other is later represented as deliberately intended at the time.

Hylophantism arose much later. The idea could only occur when the orthotypic money was much worn down : " Should the king's lytric administration declare itself prepared to replace each worn-down coin with one of full weight ? "

Emphatically no. All kings gave an unqualified refusal to replace, for in that case the whole loss through wearing down fell on the Exchequer. There would have been a negative seignorage. In order to protect the Exchequer from loss on this head the principle arose of validity by proclamation, and therewith chartalism.

The money then in circulation was left to its fate.

It may wear down as much as it likes, the king is a chartalist. How strange that the chartality of money, this achievement of exalted wisdom, this precious flower of State-ruled life, should have sprung from so base a root!

Moreover, well-meant attempts at keeping the coins up to full weight were always failing. A handful of new full-weight coins thrown into circulation cannot hold their own among much-worn money. That was indeed one of the reasons for the degrading of the hylogenic norm from time to time, though of course fiscal profit was a contributory cause.

When at last money became so much worn as to be unrecognisable, then and not till then was it decided to resort to recoining on a large scale, and the Exchequer sought to minimise its loss by debasing the coinage, *i. e.* lowering the specific content of the pieces. After this there was an interval of tranquillity.

To prevent the recurrence of such mischances, the State invented least current weight, putting a limit to the amount of abrasion allowable and, in true Treasury fashion, treating the much-worn coin, for the private possessor, as a pensatory means of payment, which the State accepted only by weight. This, though illogical, was effectual.

It was the first approach to hylophantism, for now the coins in circulation could only depart slightly from the hylogenic norm.

It was only in quite recent times, probably first in France, that the State declared its readiness to take its orthotypic money, however worn down, in accordance with the declared validity by proclamation, while it laid upon itself the rule never to put underweighted pieces in circulation.

Thus, hylophantism had with it hylodromy. The undeniable public benefit is the faultless recognisability of the pieces. It is, of course, true also that the hylic metal then has a fixed price, at any rate *ex institutione.* There were other quite unintended consequences, in which the real usefulness of hylodromy consists. The argument that under hylodromy the hylic metal becomes again a measure of value, as it is under autometallism, is not sound. The price of the hylic metal is then only fixed *ex institutione,* not *ex definitione,* and it is not true that our unit of value (mark, rouble, franc) is then defined as a given quantity of hylic metal; it is defined historically, as long as we have Chartal money. When hylodromy is praised as giving the means for a " real " definition of the unit of value, it is the true old Adam of autometallism coming out.

If one seeks counsel with the dealers for whom the hylic metal is a commodity, they are always in favour of hylodromy, for the hyloleptic administration is of the greatest convenience to them. Let us put ourselves in the place of a silver dealer, when silver is the hylic metal, or of a gold dealer, when gold.

These metals appear as bars of varying fine contents, the result of the melting down of silver plate or whatever it may be, in larger or smaller lots. The owners are ignorant, or their lots are too small for them to apply to headquarters about them. A dealer who collects all these goods, for resale at the hyloleptic office, will easily buy them up cheap (for a normal fixed price exists only for wholesale trade); and he has then an assured market for them at a fixed price. The profits, however small, are sure. Bullion dealers, therefore, can never be loud enough in their praise of hylolepsy.

There is another point advanced in favour of hylodromy, which does not, however, apply only to this special case, but to hylogenesis in general.

The State, if it strictly observes the rule only to admit hylogenic money, has a certain advantage when it replaces the original hylic metal by another, for it gives the new means of payment in exchange for the old. Let us suppose, for example, that gold replaces silver as the hylic metal. The old silver coins are handed over to the State, which gives out new gold pieces in exchange. The State therefore accumulates great stocks of silver, which now have the character of a commodity, not of a means of payment, but are saleable and form a large credit balance which can gradually be made liquid. This makes the transition easier.

There is, however, a risk in it. The stocks of the

older hylic metal are now only an ordinary commodity, though of a precious metal.   The price obtained for them depends on the market.   Precious metals *per se* are not vehicles of value, but only seem so when encased in hylogenic money.   An alteration of the hylic metal will therefore always threaten the State with loss, which is only partly covered by the commodities in stock.   So it was in Germany after 1871.

Throughout the centuries, hylogenesis, and more especially hylodromy, have shown no fitness to create a currency system faultless for all times and under all circumstances.

However improbable it seems, circumstances may compel us to remove gold from its hylic position; and this need not be due to the mere weakness of a State in temporary difficulties.

The belief that the fate of silver can never overtake gold is so prevalent because it gives such excellent support to the gold propaganda of public men. How simple and effective it is to represent the fate of silver and the assured position of gold as flowing from their very natures as metals.   But the question is not of metals but of lytric administration.   Through our lytric measures silver has lost its hylic position; therefore, in course of a long stretch of time, the same fate may overtake gold.

Even more absurd is the other idea that gold has *per se* a fixed value, and therefore must remain our measure of value; other metals do not possess this fixity, and are worthless as measures of value.

A mistake in every word.

First of all, gold is not our measure of value. In the sense here intended, we have no measure of value, for the Chartal system implies that the unit of value is only nominally, *i. e.* historically, defined. It cannot, therefore, be demanded that gold, which is not now the measure of value, should remain so. The meaning is that we should return to autometallism in gold, that is, renounce the most important achievement of economic civilisation, the chartalism of the means of payment.

The fixed price which gold has in Germany and in the neighbouring States is no property of gold, but a consequence of the hylodromic administration.

The price is only fixed even within our own borders as far as the force of our laws and ordinances extends. It is only so within our own borders between us, the citizens, and the hylic administration; for the administration itself there is no fixed price for gold.

As, between us and it, there is a fixed price now created for gold, so could it be for any metal, including silver, if this appeared expedient.

CHAPTER II

§ 6. *Classification of Kinds of Money according to their Functions*

UP to now we have classified means of payment only by their origin. The stage of Autometallism once overcome, money appears as a Chartal means of payment. At first we dealt with it as issued by the State, with a mere allusion to money not issued by the State. We then proceeded genetically with the further classification of money and obtained four kinds.

It is not asserted that as a matter of history each kind actually existed in some State or other by itself; and no preference is claimed for one of the four over the others. My endeavour is to show how they differ from one another.

How the existing currency of a State is actually organised at a given time is quite a different question. We shall assume a knowledge of primitive forms of money, and investigate how the monetary system of a State at a given time grows out of these primitive forms; for they can occur side by side. It may be that an actual monetary system exhibits

93

side by side kinds of money of fundamentally different origin. In particular hylogenic and autogenic money may very well occur in combination.

Such complex monetary systems always presuppose a series of rules, which regulate the relations of the different types of money to one another. These rules may be made by Statute, Ordinance, or Orders of the authorities.

But for our purpose all that matters is that, in some way or another, the State has made the rules : we therefore mention those " regiminal rules," or rules of administration, merely to point out that we are not distinguishing their juridical characters one from another, but only the actual effects of them. They give rise to subdivisions of monetary types which have not yet been noticed, because each kind of money has as yet been considered as existing alone.

These new subdivisions are not genetic, like the former, but functional,[1] *i. e.* they deal with the different ways in which kinds of money are used according to the kind of payment made and the legal rules affecting it. Is a particular kind of money *obligatory* or not, *definitive* or not, and finally is it *valuta* or not ? These are technical terms to be explained.

If, as the Metallists do, we recognise as legitimate

[1] We are asking not how they came there, but what they do when they are there.—TR.

only one type, namely, the hylogenic-orthotypic, our task would be simpler; but we aim not at a simple theory but an adequate one. It is not our fault if States for historical reasons possess complicated monetary systems, and, in such, the question at once arises, Where is the line to be drawn? What forms part of the monetary system of the State and what does not? We must not make our definition too narrow.

The criterion cannot be that the money is issued by the State, for that would exclude kinds of money which are of the highest importance; I refer to bank-notes: they are not issued by the State, but they form a part of its monetary system. Nor can legal tender be taken as the test, for in monetary systems there are very frequently kinds of money which are not legal tender (*e.g.* in Germany (1905) Treasury notes [1] are not legal tender).

We keep most closely to the facts if we take as our test, that the money is accepted in payments made to the State's offices. Then all means by which a payment can be made to the State form part of the monetary system. On this basis it is not the issue, but the *acceptation,* as we call it, which is decisive. State acceptation delimits the monetary system. By the expression " State-acceptation " is to be understood only the acceptance at State pay offices where the State is the recipient.

[1] *Reichskassenscheine,* Imperial Treasury Warrants.

But, since the State pay offices are not all important, and include, for example, even the booking offices of State railways, be it said that only the large State pay offices are meant, and particularly those which take part in lytric administration under the direction of the State. For instance, in Germany a great part of the lytric administration is in the hands of the Reichsbank [1] (the precise nature of this institution does not matter), and for the Reichsbank, which is very far from being a merely private bank, the administrative rules are framed with particular precision.

The easiest way to reach our goal, which is the functional classification of kinds of money, is to distinguish whether or not the State takes part in a payment and, if so, in what way it does so. Payments to which the State is a party, either as giver or receiver, will be called *centric*, because the State is regarded as the centre from which the ordering of the business of payment radiates. Payments in which the State takes no part either as giver or receiver we call *paracentric*; such are all payments between private persons. From the systematic point of view they are not so important as is generally supposed, for they mostly, so to speak, regulate themselves.

Centric payments are either: (1) payments to the State as receiver; these we call *epicentric*.

Accepting a means of payment in an epicentric

[1] Imperial Bank.

payment means, as we have already said, State acceptation.

Or they are : (2) payments made by the State, these we will call *apocentric*. They are of the greatest importance in the functional classification, and it is very remarkable that hitherto they have been so little studied that they have gone without a name.

We have accordingly the following classification :

Payments are

either centric   or paracentric,

either   or
epicentric   apocentric

anepicentric.

By these characteristics the functional rules regulating the internal monetary system of a State can be easily drawn out.

The most usual functional classification of money is whether it is legal tender or not. Of course this relates only to those payments which are not epicentric; for we have taken the obligation to accept in epicentric payments as the criterion for State money. When to this is added the obligation to accept for anepicentric payments, the money becomes legal tender for all purposes. In this case we will call the money *obligatory*, but, if it is not legal tender for anepicentric payments, so that the recipient's consent is necessary, then the money is *facultative*.

H

In this it has been tacitly assumed that the payment to be made is not smaller than the value of the piece of money which is tendered. For, in law, it is always the duty of the payer to procure such pieces of money as are precisely equal to the sum to be paid. It is never the duty of the recipient to give change, though he very often voluntarily does so.

In Germany the gold pieces in 1905 were obligatory money, but the thalers were so as well, because legally one was bound to accept them. This does not imply that there was no functional difference between the gold pieces and the thalers—only that the difference did not consist in the legal obligation to accept them, for this was common to both (in 1905).

In Austria from 1857 the silver gulden were obligatory money, but from 1866 the State notes, and even the bank-notes, were also legal tender, for they were legal tender for anepicentric payments, and therefore for all and sundry payments.

The subdivision of money into obligatory and facultative—or, more precisely, into money which it is obligatory or facultative for the receiver to accept —is totally independent of the question whether specie or notal money is under consideration. By *notal* we mean what we above called *paratypic*; our thalers were notal, but yet obligatory; the Austrian notes were, as their name shows, notal—but they were obligatory money. So it is with the other subdivisions already discussed.

The question whether certain kinds of money are obligatory or facultative depends on the amount of the payment. The law draws the line, or fixes a " critical " amount. For example, in Germany by law silver coins were obligatory for payments of twenty marks and under, the nickel and copper pieces obligatory for payments of one mark and under. Both kinds were facultative for payments which exceeded the critical amount. But it is important to remember that we are referring to anepicentric payments (*i.e.* apocentric or paracentric); for it is fundamental that epicentric payments can be made by means of such kinds of money to an unlimited amount. If there are exceptions to this rule they come from the absent-mindedness of the legislator.

We had money which was obligatory *per se* and money which was facultative *per se ;* in Germany the Treasury notes, which were not legal tender for anepicentric payments, belonged to this class; and finally there were kinds of money either obligatory or facultative according to the amount of the anepicentric payment.

In Germany those kinds of money, of which the obligatory or facultative property depended upon a " critical " amount, were usually called parting-money [1] or small change, and, since we have only coined money of this kind, we talk of it as small

<hr>
[1] *Scheide-geld.*

coin. We shall adopt this popular expression, defining
" small change " once for all as a functional concept,
not in itself necessary, but adopted here as use
and wont. Sometimes small change includes a kind
of money which we have already come to know in
our genetic classification, viz. coined autogenetic
money. Anyone who adopts this terminology must
reckon our thalers as small change. But in order
to avoid all ambiguity, we, as we have said, lay
down once for all that we use " small change " as a
functional concept applying to those kinds of money
of which the obligatory or facultative property is
determined by a " critical " amount. In Austria
there are examples of paper small change, so that
it is not sufficient to speak of small " coin."

After " small change," we must come to a
reckoning with " current money," which is usually
contrasted with the notion of small change.

This is a consequence of the earlier undeveloped
monetary system; in it we go back to a time when
in the State monetary system only the two following
kinds of money were represented : orthotypic-hylogenic on the one hand, and metalloplatic-autogenic
on the other. There was no papyroplatic-autogenic
money; either because it did not exist, or because
people were afraid to recognise it as a constituent part
of the State money.

In such a simple monetary system the metallo-
platic-autogenetic money had usually the functional

status of what we call small change; and since
there was only one other kind of money, the
orthotypic-hylogenic money was denominated current money; and the classification at that time was
exhaustive.

But to-day such a simple classification is no longer
possible, and it is astonishing that the attempt is
made to go on working with such an undeveloped
terminology, when its basis, in the old simple system
of State money, has long since been destroyed.

Our classification into obligatory and facultative
money, with due respect for the existence or non-
existence of a critical limit of amount, is entirely
suitable to the present highly-developed monetary
system. If we wish to make use of the concept
" current money " we must come to an understanding about it. It answers our purpose best to take
current money to be a functional (not a genetic) kind
of money, as we have done in the case of small change.
We will define current money to be that kind of
money which is obligatory *per se* without regard to
the amount of the payment. Austrian State notes
(and the bank-notes too) were current money; and
so were English bank-notes. The Austrian silver
gulden were current money, and so were English
sovereigns. There is no risk of confusion, because in
another place we shall duly introduce the remaining
distinguishing properties.

According to the obligation to receive it in

anepicentric payments we then get the following functional classification of monies :

Irrespective of the amount of the payment.		According to the amount of the payment.	
Obligatory.	Facultative.	Obligatory.	Facultative.
Current money.	Purely facultative money.	Small change.	

This survey shows that a place must be kept for purely facultative money, or there would be no place for Treasury notes, which are neither small change nor current money.

An entirely different but equally functional classification of money is based on the convertibility of State-accepted money.

In the monetary system of a State there must be one kind of money which is definitive, as opposed to provisional (convertible) money. Thus there must be at least one kind that is inconvertible—to describe it negatively. Money is definitive if, when payment is made in it, the business is completely concluded : first for the payer, secondly for the recipient, and thirdly for the issuer of the money. The payer is no longer under an obligation, the recipient has no further rights either against the payer or against the State, if the State has issued the money.

Now this is not the case with provisional (convertible) money. If the payment is made in convertible money, it is true that the recipient has no further claim against the payer, but he still has it against the issuer of the money; he can demand from the issuer the same quantity of definitive money. If the State is the issuer, the State remains engaged to redeem; if not the State, an institution, say a Bank; then the private issuer is and remains under an obligation to redeem.

In Germany the Treasury notes were issued by the State; a private person was not obliged to accept them; if he did so, they were convertible, and therefore not definitive money. On the other hand, our gold pieces are definitive money; the State is under no obligation to give other kinds of money for them.

In this way we obtain the second of our functional subdivisions; it, too, is quite independent of the genetic divisions. We do not ask whether the money is hylogenic or not, but what are the mutual relations between the kinds of money occurring in the system. Inconvertible State notes, as they usually were in Austria, belonged entirely to the class of definitive money, which is by no means a statement in their favour. Our thalers too would be classified as definitive money, if all depended on the laws; but since in the administration of the laws the thalers were in fact converted, and since we judge according to administered law, it follows that our thalers were convertible.

There are two kinds of convertibility : direct and indirect. For direct conversion there are offices bound to carry out the exchange; conversion is indirect when a kind of money may be paid in without limit, but may be refused for apocentric payments. The indirect conversion of our thalers would have still continued if the direct exchange had been refused, but in 1905 (see Karl Helfferich) both kinds of conversion existed side by side.

The third functional subdivision of money appears in apocentric payments. It relates only to definitive money and has nothing to do with provisional (convertible) money. There can be more than one kind of definitive money, as, for example, in Germany both gold pieces and thalers were at one time legally definitive. In France both the gold pieces and the silver five-franc pieces are definitive. In which of the definitive kinds are the apocentric payments made ? The State adopts the principle that it can choose which it likes.

In Austria, where before 1892 the silver gulden were equally definitive with the State notes, the question arose in which kind of money the State should pay : as is well known, it did not choose silver gulden.

If there is only one kind of definitive money, the State can, it is true, also tender provisional money for its apocentric payments, but in the last resort it can only insist on paying in definitive money.

From this arises the most important of the sub-divisions stated here. That kind of definitive money which is always kept ready and can be insisted on for apocentric payments (if they exceed the critical limit) we call *valuta*; all other kinds of money (without regard to the amount) we call *accessory*.

Putting aside small change, which is always accessory, we get the following scheme of classification :

Acceptance obligatory.			Acceptance facultative.
Definitive money.		Provisional money.	
Enforced by the State.	Not enforced by the State.		
Valuta money.	Accessory money (Small change also comes here).		

In Germany the State did not treat the thalers as if it could force people to take them in its apocentric payments, although legally it could. So that in Germany thalers were not valuta money.

In France (1803 to 1870) the State at certain periods kept the silver five-franc pieces in hand for its (apocentric) payments, and compelled people to take them; in that case they were valuta. At other times it did the same with the gold pieces; in that case the gold pieces were valuta. Yet all the time both kinds were obligatory and definitive.

Accordingly, the question before us is, What kind of definitive money is, in fact, kept in hand for apocentric payments? It is not what the law offers as possible, but only what the Government selects, and for this kind of money we use the expression " valuta." Everywhere there is a valuta or standard money. This conception too is entirely functional. Standard money can be hylogenic or autogenic, it can be managed hylodromically or not; but all this does not matter from the functional point of view.

The concept " valuta money " is a sub-class of definitive money; first of all, the requirements of ultimate validity must be satisfied, and then, secondly, the money must be held in readiness for apocentric payments. This second is the business of the State, a regulation of lytric administration; it is not inferred from legal regulations, but from the facts which help to determine their administration. Having the money in stock is a political and not a juridical matter; it often depends not on the State's wishes, but on its powers. Having the money in stock is a question of power which influences politics and therefore has a determining influence on administration. If the State has simply not the power to hold in stock the particular kind of money recommended by the wisdom of skilled advisers as the best, it disregards the advisers, and merely holds whatever, in the circumstances, is within reach.

The concept of valuta money cannot be arrived at merely from Acts of Parliament; but it can be found without difficulty from the point of view of the administration. That is the only explanation which fits the facts. It is of no use to ask censoriously whether the State itself is observing the law or not. The State is not, in fact, bound by its laws, which it only maintains for its subjects : from time to time it of itself creates new rights and obligations to meet the facts administratively, and perhaps afterwards changes the law to make it correspond. We neither commend nor defend this proceeding, but only call attention to it as a fact of political experience. The person who will not see this cannot comprehend the most important events in the history of money.

In Germany our gold pieces were valuta, not because they were made of gold, nor because they were hylodromic, but only because the State, when it made a payment, was ready in the last resort to pay in gold pieces, and, if it found it at all inconvenient, totally to refuse any other means of payment which the recipient might happen to want. But though the other means of payment—*e.g.* thalers or notes— were convenient, and the State did not refuse to pay in them, it did not enforce receipt of them, but was always prepared to pay in gold coin.

If it happened that the price of silver was about as high as it was in 1860, it would be very inconvenient for the State to pay in thalers, and it would at once decline to do so.

In Germany in 1905 thalers were definitive but not valuta money. Our gold pieces were valuta money, because they were not only definitive but also always kept in stock for apocentric payments.

In Austria about 1870, for example, in addition to the silver gulden the inconvertible paper State notes were also definitive. But which of these were valuta? The State, from force of circumstances, was then entirely averse from paying in silver gulden. Hence at that time the silver gulden, though definitive, were not valuta money; on the other hand, the State notes, in spite of being papyroplatic-autogenic money, were nevertheless valuta; for the State held them in readiness for its payments. We shall find that the bank-notes too were valuta.

Kinds of money which are not valuta we will call accessory. A kind of money is accessory first when it is not valuta, so that it can be refused; secondly, when it is obligatory, but at the same time redeemable, so that it is not definitive; thirdly, when it is definitive but not forced on the recipient in apocentric payments. Throughout we always refer to payments above the critical limit, because it is only such payments which are important for the concept of valuta money.

Our Treasury notes were accessory because they were redeemable. Our thalers, even when they were inconvertible from the administrative standpoint, remained accessory as long as the State did not force them on the recipient.

In Austria about 1870 the silver gulden were completely accessory, for the State did not hold them in readiness for apocentric payments in spite of the intention of the monetary system of 1857 to give the silver gulden the position of valuta. We do not regard good intentions. Was the State, in fact, prepared to pay in silver gulden? In 1870 it was not. From political causes the silver gulden had, in fact, lost their position as valuta and had become accessory, however much we may regret the fact. The administrative point of view which is put forward here must be maintained throughout, however much we may dislike what has happened, for example, in Austria. Regulations are not based merely on law, but on human powers and political situations.

This, of course, is not jurisprudence, bound to adhere to a given regulation; but it is politics, and money matters are in the domain of politics.

An insight into the nature of valuta money is of the greatest importance, amongst other things, because of the bearing of it on business. When the State determines to fulfil its obligations in such and such a kind of money, it might appear as if it were only pronouncing on the one matter of its own apocentric payments, while other payments were not affected. For example, if the Austrian Treasury announced that it made its payments in State notes, one might suppose that this did not affect paracentric payments. Among private individuals a lytric debt can then still be conceived as a debt in silver gulden, because this kind of money was valuta according to the law of 1857, while the State notes were first issued in 1866. This largely sentimental view is quite wrong, for as soon as the State has elevated a kind of money (say the State notes) into the position of valuta, it cannot in its judicial capacity require that the private debtor should perform his lytric obligations in one way and the State as debtor in another. So, if from political necessity the State announces that henceforth it will pay in State notes, as fountain of law it must equally allow the State notes to suffice for other payments. And indeed not only in epicentric payments but in paracentric payments, when there is a dispute the State must decide as a judge that a payment in State notes is sufficient. If it did not, it would, as judge, be condemning its own course of action, and contradicting itself.

The consequence is, in a legal dispute the means of payment which the creditor is compelled to accept is always that which the State has put in the position of valuta. The judicial decision is final. Apart from friendly agreement, all payments eventually have to be made in valuta money. Consequently lytric obligations are always drawn out in valuta money, unless previously, by agreement, the accessory kinds of money are accepted by the parties. An obligation expressed in marks, francs or roubles signifies an obligation to be performed in the then existing valuta money of the countries concerned.

Valuta money then is simply money; for the foreign observer, the fate of the unit of value of a country depends on the fate of the valuta money in its lytric administration.

The laws do not decide what shall be valuta money, they merely express a pious hope, for they are powerless against their creator, the State; the State in its payments decides what is valuta money and the Law Courts follow suit. Not lytric regulations but sovereign power prescribes the money of apocentric payments, and the lytric administration adjusts itself accordingly.

For this reason the valuta money is the pivot of the whole lytric organisation, though jurisprudence cannot allow this, being bound to the formally subsisting laws. Valuta money is the result of political considerations, and this is the clue to the mysterious development of lytric history.

The valuta means of payment of a country are called " standard " in the narrower sense of the word. In its larger sense " standard " often denotes the whole of the lytric machinery of the country.

To find out what is " standard " in the narrower

sense we always have to ask the two questions : which kinds of money are definitive? and which of the definitive kinds does the State force on the creditor in apocentric payments?

The standard is not simply current money, for there is current money which is not definitive. Nor is it current coin; for this would exclude paper, while there are paper standards. Nor is it possible to start from the question, What metals are employed in a hylic manner? for there are standards without the hylic metals. Lastly, the standard cannot be ascertained from the law, for the question which definitive kind of money the State employs apocentrically is one of fact. The functional classification of money, especially the most important one into valuta and accessory, is totally independent of the genetic classification, especially of that into specie and notal money, so that we may assert, accessory money may be specie or notal, valuta money may be specie or notal.

It is hard for the metallists to recognise that specie money may turn out to be accessory; but the understanding of the most important historical events rests entirely on this. We must here, as always, keep our wishes quite separate from our observations. The metallist, in his great enthusiasm for specie, will, even when it has become accessory, still trace in it a lingering influence—he remains true to his first love.

Similarly he cannot with all his heart recognise

that valuta money is occasionally notal. Notal money, because he hates it, seems to him to be unworthy and even incapable of such a pre-eminent position, and he talks of " anomalous developments."

But we have no such prejudices. So long as we are only describing, we take it as an axiom, that money can be regarded genetically or functionally; in this way we are led to classifications which are independent of each other. There can be specie money which is either valuta or accessory; notal money which is either valuta or accessory.

We do not deny that it may be better if the valuta money is specie and the accessory notal, but this consideration is for public men, not theorists.

§ 7. *Bimetallism and Types of Standard*

In classifying the monetary systems of different countries we must start from the valuta money, leaving the accessory alone for a little.

The first question, then, is whether in a particular country the valuta money is specie or not. If it is specie there are the further questions, what is the hylic metal, and whether there is complete hylodromy or not.

If the valuta money is notal, the question may be asked, What is the money made of?

There are metalloplatic and papyroplatic notal money systems, with or without hylodromy.

The so-called paper money system, which is the most feared, is the papyroplatic system without hylodromy.

When valuta money is only considered genetically the concepts of monometallism and bimetallism do not arise. Valuta money is determined by the action of the State in regard to its own (apocentric) payments. To discuss monometallism and bimetallism, we must survey the entire monetary system of the State and the various kinds of definitive money. The concept of definitive money is a broader notion than valuta; all valuta money is definitive, but all definitive money is not valuta.

Monometallism exists if there is only one definitive kind of money and that hylogenic. The most important cases are : silver alone is hylic (*monargyrism*), or gold alone is hylic (*monochrysism*). This does not mean that monargyric silver money is valuta; it may be accessory, but only that no metal except silver is hylic. Similarly with monochrysic money; it can be employed as valuta or accessory; but no metal other than gold is hylic.

In Austria from 1857 there was monargyrism, for silver was the only hylic metal; only silver could without any limitation be transformed into money, namely, silver gulden. But, as is well known, silver money during the period was not valuta; it was accessory, for the notes of the bank (to be mentioned later) were valuta, and from 1866 onwards the State notes were so as well. So that monargyrism tells us nothing about the standard, but merely asserts that one metal only, and that silver, is hylic.

The metallists, as is well known, have not sufficiently recognised the functional subdivisions of money, and so have failed to make the distinction between valuta and accessory money.

In Germany before 1871 the matter was simpler; we had monargyrism, and the monargyric silver money was valuta.

Since 1871 monochrysism existed, and at the same time the monochrysic money was valuta (1905).

Similarly in England, at the time of the Napoleonic wars, monochrysism existed. Only gold could be turned into money; silver, which already in the eighteenth century had ceased to be hylic, could not. But at that time the monochrysic money was not valuta, but accessory. The position was exactly similar to that in Austria from 1857 to 1879, except that gold and silver as hylic metals changed places.

There is *bimetallism*, when two hylic metals (say gold and silver) are allowed to exist side by side.

Silver can be turned into definitive money without any limit; so also can gold. That is the nature of bimetallism.

Since each of the two kinds of money, argyrogenic as well as chrysogenic, are legally definitive, it follows on principle that one kind is not convertible in terms of the other. The definitive silver money is not officially convertible into gold money, nor the definitive gold money into silver money. The two have no functional relation to one another; they exist independently side by side.

Bimetallism cannot be defined by means of current money, *i. e.* money which is legal tender for all purposes; nor can hylogenic current money be taken as a basis, for such money may be redeemable and therefore is not always definitive. This is generally overlooked because current money is not usually distinguished from definitive money. As is well known, France introduced a bimetallic monetary system in 1803, and the States of the Latin Union adopted this system. It is true that in these States silver and gold current money are in use side by side, but the essence of the matter is that these States possess argyrogenic and chrysogenic money side by side as definitive money. Furthermore, it is not true that France after 1876 (when the free coinage of silver was discontinued) still continued to have bimetallism in the sense of the law of 1803 : silver then ceased to be hylic and gold alone remained hylic. Bimetallism consequently ceased. Since 1876 France has had a monochrysic monetary system, and in addition it has, in its five-franc pieces, an argyroplatic money, which is no longer argyrogenic, but an argyroplatic-autogenic money.

It is true that the silver five-franc pieces are legal

tender for all purposes and thus are current money, and that they have even remained definitive; but they are not definitive and also hylogenic, like the gold money.

French writers, it is true, maintain that bimetallism continued after 1876, but they have not the same notion of their system as we have; they cling to the idea of general legal tender, and know nothing of definitive money, nor of hylogenesis.

On the other hand, the bimetallism of 1803, in our sense of the term, did not experience the smallest interruption through the Franco-German War, for it is a hylic, not a functional phenomenon. During the war the notes of the Bank became valuta, but after it, just as before, money could be produced without limit from both silver and gold; so that bimetallism continued. The only difference was that another equally definitive kind of money (bank-notes), which was autogenic, appeared by its side, and this kind of money became valuta, whereas both the kinds of bimetallic money became accessory.

In the period from 1803 to 1870—if we ignore the revolution of 1848—the conditions were simpler. There was always a hylogenic money which was valuta, either gold money or silver money; but the choice between the two kinds of money was a matter for the administration; it was not regulated by law, which did no more than put both kinds of hylogenic money at the disposal of the State for its apocentric

payments.   Whichever kind was selected was for the
time being valuta and the other accessory.   Bimetallism then leaves it undetermined whether one of its
kinds of money shall be valuta or not, and which
of them shall be valuta, or whether perchance (as in
France in 1870) a third kind shall intrude itself as
such.

The French Government, as is well known, chose
silver money to use as valuta from 1803 to about
1860, and after 1860 gold money; this made no alteration in the bimetallic system, which only came to an
end when silver lost its hylic property.   The reasons
which moved the State at one time to treat silver and
at another time gold as valuta do not concern us,
for they arise out of lytric policy.   Effects on the
relative prices of the two precious metals will not be
considered here.

The reproach is often levelled against bimetallism
that gold and silver cannot at one and the same time
be measures of value—a strange objection which can
only be understood from the standpoint of autometallism.   Under all conditions the constitution of bimetallism is Chartalist, not pensatory, and least of all bi-
autometallistic; and neither merely gold nor merely
silver is employed in it as the measure of value.
The unit of value is always the franc, and it is a matter
of complete indifference for the internal trade of
France which kind of money is valuta.   At a given
moment there is always in use only one kind of valuta

money, not two kinds side by side, so that France never had a gold standard and a silver standard at the same time, but either the one or the other, except in the unsettled times when a third form of standard was chosen.

In France bimetallism was so arranged that hylodromy was provided for both hylic metals; but so that both hylodromies should not exist together, there was hylodromy only for the hylic metal of the valuta money for the time being. It is easy to see the reason for this. Hylodromy proceeds from the conjunction of *hylolepsy* and *hylophantism.* There can be hylolepsy in both accessory and valuta money; hylophantism only in valuta money (although not always even there), for it arises from the lytric metal being obtainable without limit.

From 1803 it was laid down : first that definitive money could be made of silver, and secondly that any quantity of silver delivered was convertible into definitive money. This is *argyrolepsy.* Further, worn silver coins were always withdrawn by the State pay-offices, so that the coins in circulation always remained of full weight. On the other hand, these full-weight silver coins were only obtainable with certainty when the State treated the silver money as valuta, so that argyrophantism only existed during the periods when the silver money was valuta, and only during these periods was there argyrodromy.

Similarly, from 1803 it was laid down that definitive

money could be made of gold and that any quantity of gold which was offered was convertible into definitive money. This is *chrysolepsy*. Further, worn gold coins were withdrawn by the State, so that those in circulation always remained of full weight. On the other hand, these full-weight gold coins were only obtainable with certainty (without the help of a money changer) when the State treated gold coin as valuta, so that chrysophantism only existed during the periods when the gold money was valuta, and only during these periods was there chrysodromy.

Combining both together, hylolepsy always exists for both metals, but hylophantism only for the hylic metal of which the valuta money is for the time being composed.

In any case there was complete hylodromy for the money which was for the time being valuta, but only hylolepsy for the money which was for the time being accessory.

I do not conceive this to be a necessary property of bimetallism, and therefore only say, that in the sense used above, it was so in France.

The hylic metal of the money which for the time being was valuta had a price confined between very narrow limits. On the other hand, the hylic metal of the money which for the time being was accessory had only a lower price limit; it had no upper price limit.

All this only applies to the interior of the State and

to the customers of the lytric administration of the State, but not to the lytric administration itself.

During the war of 1870, when both kinds of money had ceased to be valuta (in favour of the bank-notes), there was for both metals only hylolepsy, not hylophantism.

Similarly in the case of monometallism, hylodromy is only a possible epiphenomenon, not a necessary requisite.

The money systems of different countries can be classified according to the genetic, platic, and dromic quality of the kind of money which is valuta. The survey is made easier if we take the specie constitution (*i. e.* the hylogenic orthotypic constitution). We then obtain the following most important types.

I. The valuta money is in specie; then distinguish :

1. Silver, the hylic metal.

This describes the English monetary system from William the Conqueror till far into the eighteenth century, for the gold coins (called guineas, 1663) were at first accessory. The hylogenic norm of the valuta silver coins was often altered and the specific content debased, but this did not touch the essence of the specie constitution.

From 1803 to about 1860 France had a similar monetary system, for apocentric payments were made in silver money, the gold money admitted beside it being accessory.

Before 1871 the German States of the Customs Union had a similar system.

(*a*) In England argyrodromy was not carried out, because in former times the full weight of the valuta silver pieces in circulation was not kept up, if we judge full weight by the hylogenic norm in force for the time being. There was therefore a silver standard in the hylic and platic but not in the dromic sense of the word.

(*b*) In France, and practically in Germany as well, the silver standard was also dromic.

Austria too, in accordance with the law of 1857, had this system during the last months of the year 1858.

2. Gold, the hylic metal.

In the course of the eighteenth century England went over to this system, when the apocentric payments were made in guineas, by an administrative act, at what precise date is not ascertainable. The earlier silver coins were retained as accessory (small change).

About 1860 this system was introduced into France, through the administrative procedure which made apocentric payments in gold. After the interruption of the war of 1870–71, a gold standard was again tried (1876); or rather silver was next deprived of its hylic position. The stocks of silver coins were made " notal," and there was sometimes a gold standard (when the apocentric payments were made in gold coins).

In Germany in 1871 preparation was made for this system; and about 1876 it was completed, when apocentric payments were made in gold coins.

(*a*) In England the chrysodromy was imperfect so long as the apocentric payments were made even in worn gold coins.

(*b*) In France and Germany there was approximately complete chrysodromy, for worn pieces never made their appearance in apocentric payments.

II. When the valuta money is Notal, quite different standard types arise. By Notal is meant the opposite to specie; it is what we have called paratypic (p. 70).

1. Metalloplatic money.

In France after 1876 the apocentric payments were at times made in the silver money (five-franc pieces) which had become notal. These were metalloplatic but not specie payments.

In Holland the silver money (Dutch gulden), which had long since become notal, appears to have been employed as regular valuta. The valuta money was not, therefore, specie, though metalloplatic.

(*a*) In the French case the usual chrysodromy was interrupted, or at any rate (on account of the premium on gold) altered in relation to the price limits of gold.

(*b*) In the Dutch case chrysodromy appears to have been practically maintained, indirectly through exodromic administration.

2. Papyroplatic money.

Valuta paper money occurred in England during

the Napoleonic Wars, when the notes of the Bank became valuta through the suspension of specie payments; that is to say, the guinea was dethroned as valuta, but remained as accessory. So in France during the war of 1870–71.

In Austria from the beginning of the year 1859 this state of affairs lasted a long time and, strictly speaking, did so still in 1905 so long as apocentric payments could not certainly be made in the new gold money (of the law of 1892).

(*a*) In England and France during those years of war, hylodromy was completely lost.

(*b*) But this is not necessarily the case with valuta paper money. In Austria it is true that chrysodromy —the goal in view—did not come into being immediately after 1892, but, as in Holland, only after some years (through exodromic administration). So in Russia.

We can now distinguish no less than eight types of standard :

$$
\begin{array}{llll}
\text{I} & 1a & \text{I} & 2a \\
\text{I} & 1b & \text{I} & 2b \\
\multicolumn{2}{c}{\underbrace{\hphantom{xxxxx}}_{\text{Specie}}} & \multicolumn{2}{c}{}
\end{array}
\qquad
\begin{array}{llll}
\text{II} & 1a & \text{II} & 2a \\
\text{II} & 1b & \text{II} & 2b \\
\multicolumn{2}{c}{\underbrace{\hphantom{xxxxx}}_{\text{Notal}}} & \multicolumn{2}{c}{}
\end{array}
$$

four of which belong to a specie system and the other four to a notal system.

The common subdivision of standards derived merely from the platic quality of the valuta money (gold, silver, paper) is, as we see, quite inadequate.

And in this connection we ought not to speak of a double standard, since that describes the whole monetary system, leaving it undetermined which kind of money is valuta. Similarly the expression parallel standard relates to the whole monetary system, which recognises one kind of valuta money for certain dealings and another kind for other dealings, while we are always thinking of a state of things in which only one kind of money is valuta. Even the so-called "limping standard" does not designate a peculiar standard in our sense of the term, but a special condition of the whole monetary system. The term implies that the valuta money is specie and that, beside it, there is allowed as accessory a special kind of money, namely, metalloplatic metal money for definitive—but not valuta—use, and once part of a specie system. Since Germany has had a gold standard the thalers have fallen into this position. During the periods when France had a gold standard the silver five-franc pieces were in this condition. Assuming that in Austria the gold standard was already carried through, the retained silver gulden were in that accessory position. This condition of the monetary system becomes very striking during the transition to a gold standard, but has logically nothing to do with the gold standard. Go back to the time (before 1860) when France had a silver standard; if the free coinage of gold had been discontinued, but the gold coin had been retained as definitive money, then the gold coins would have become notal and taken the position later conceded to the silver five-franc pieces. Then there would have been a limping silver standard, just as at certain times there was a limping gold standard.

The limping condition implies, further, that the money retained as accessory has a negative agio (to be described later), for if it had a positive agio it would vanish automatically from circulation, being saleable at a profit as a commodity.

If, owing to a (very improbable) rise in the price of silver, the thalers in Germany or the five-franc pieces in France were to acquire a positive agio, these coins would then, it is true, still remain notal, but they would no longer have a negative agio and the limping would vanish. Remember that the notal character frequently, but not essentially, implies a value less than the face value. A notal system is the opposite to a specie system. Whether a notal accessory money is under value, of full value, or over value is, as we shall see, a separate question which is only concerned with the metallic worth of the pieces in comparison with the value as money.

In our classification of standards we have been considering only the valuta money, not the whole monetary system, and so have left out accessory money. At first the classification only views the relation towards metals; when this relation changes, the standard changes. But the relation is very complex. If there is a lytric metal, *i. e.* if the valuta money is hylogenic, then (as in mediæval England) the hylogenic norm can change. This is a change of standard in spite of the identity of the hylic metal; the change is then confined to the norm.

But it is also possible to change over from one hylic metal to another, *e. g.* from silver to gold, a hylic change; or the hylic metal can be dropped altogether and we go over to autogenic money.

Conceivably, too, the hylic metal and the hylogenic norm are retained while the constitution of the pieces changes,—a platic change. It would occur, for instance, if our lytric administration accepted without limit a pound of gold at the rate of 1395 marks, but only paid this price in silver coins or notes.

Finally, a complete hylodromy can be introduced where it did not exist before, or can be dropped where it had formerly existed; or the limits of the price of the hylic metal which had previously been customary can be altered. All these would be dromic changes.

The changes in the norm and the hylic, platic and dromic changes may be independent or may cross each other. A change can conceivably be made from silver to gold as the hylic metal, and at the same time from silver coins to paper.

Our metallistic theorists almost always adhere to the platic point of view; it is only since Bamberger's labours that the dromic point of view has been at all accurately developed, unhappily without an appropriate terminology. The hylic relations were entirely unrecognised. The changes in the norm excited the greatest attention, because people did not recognise that the value of our money depends on what it is proclaimed to be.

For the champion of the Chartal theory all this discussion has less importance than for the metallists, but it still has a little from the light it throws on historical development.

§ 8a.   *Bank-notes*

Means of payment, accepted by our State, *i. e.* allowed for epicentric payments, are assumed to be issued by the State; and usually are so. But they may have been issued by a foreign State and through "acceptation" received into our system of State means of payment. For example, the Austrian thalers, certainly issued by a foreign State, were by acceptation incorporated into the German monetary system.

If, however, we assume issue by the State, it is impossible for us to discover one very widespread means of payment, *i. e.* bank-notes, for whatever they may be, they are not issued by the State, and so, in any case, are not included in the means of payment issued by the State.

Our Treasury notes and the Austrian State notes are issued by the State, but bank-notes are created and put in circulation by the Bank, not by the State;

so they lack the quality of being issued by the State.

To explain this phenomenon we must first of all say what a bank is. If at first we entirely disregard its relation to the State (which often comes in later), a bank is a private undertaking for profit, which carries on a strictly defined kind of business. But, because its activities are at the same time undeniably beneficial to the public, the State, with all its restrictions and supervision, takes pains to give them its powerful support.

The banks which interest us here are essentially limited to the so-called Discount and Lombard (or Lending) business; they also carry on Giro (or Circulation) business, and the purchase and sale of Government securities on behalf of their customers. Banking as a Discount and Lombard business assumes that there are people who wish to obtain loans on the security of movable property. Certain kinds of goods, certain kinds of paper (*e. g.* State bonds), are allowed as security.

In this so-called Lombard business the bank naturally requires interest on the advances which it makes; and, if they are not repaid at the proper time, the bank reimburses itself by realising the security. Under expert management advances are perfectly safe and highly profitable. Everyone who carries on almost any kind of business may find himself in a position when he requires an advance for a short time.

K

The business of a bank further concerns what are called "Bills of Exchange." The exact nature of Bills of Exchange is a matter of commercial law. A bill is a debt warrant to which the law gives special privileges. It is expressed in units of means of payment which are valuta when the contrary is not stated. Someone is under an obligation to pay the sum stated on the face of the document at a fixed time : at first to a person named as creditor, but subsequently to every other person to whom the rights of the original creditor have been assigned in a particular manner. Such bills form the basis of the Discount business of the bank, which is as follows :

The creditor drawing the bill, if he wishes to get cash for the money owed to him at once, although the debt is payable in the future, offers the bill to the bank, that it may take over his rights and pay him the amount at once, of course with a discount. The bank does this, earns so much per cent. by means of the Discount, and at maturity receives the whole sum which formerly was due to the drawer. The bank has discounted the bill. The business is very safe, for naturally the solvency of the debtor is ascertained at the outset.

This outline, recalling familiar facts, may be enough to show what the banks in question really are. Their extremely important and very responsible business (the honourable management of which is the pride of all civilised States) seems a mystery only because its technical terms are but little current with the public and the handling of huge sums of money is confusing to the man in the street. Fundamentally they deal in pledges and advances, and, when such businesses are carried on in a small way, they are wrapped in no mystery.

A bank, such as we have described, can obviously only be started if the undertaking has at its disposal a certain stock of State-issued money. But since the rate of interest for Lombard loans and discounts is not very high, the profits of our bank, though sure, are not great in comparison with the invested capital. One way of increasing them is by the issue of notes. The bank makes notes and offers them in payment to its customers. Issuing notes is not a special business, carried on in conjunction with the other businesses of the bank, but a special way in which the bank endeavours to make its payments, which themselves arise out of its general business. It tries to pay in its own notes instead of in money issued by the State, because then with a comparatively small capital it can make greater profits than it otherwise could.

But what is a bank-note ? The usual definition is : a document by which the bank promises to pay the holder at sight such and such a sum of money. " At sight " means when the holder tenders or presents the document for this purpose.

The money means money issued by the State, ultimately the money which is for the time being valuta. The bank does not promise to pay in metallic money. Generally the sum is stated in the usual units of the country (marks, francs, roubles), and it is for the lytric administration of the State to determine what kind of money is for the time being valuta.

Even if metal money was stated on the face of the document itself, this would be of none effect against any changes which had occurred in valuta, for such changes affect all lytric obligations, those of the bank included.

Bank-notes, then, are a promise to pay a sum expressed in valuta money. In fact usually the document states, " The bank will pay the holder at sight so many units of value."

But, if the manager of a bank writes out such a document in his own hand, so that its legal validity is indisputable, is that a bank-note? According to present ideas it is not. Such a document has not only to be valid at law, but also must be made in a definite external form, which has previously been precisely laid down. The document must be chartal to make the genuineness quickly recognisable. A bank-note, then, is a chartal promise to pay given by a bank.

But is it really a promise to pay? Naturally only effective promises to pay are in question. Is it one?

It is easy to answer, " Of course it is, for it is stated on the face of the document." Yet this answer is wrong. At the most the statement on the note shows that it was intended as a promise to pay when

it was made.   But we want to know if it is effective
now, and what is written on it gives us no information
on this point, because it is of a past date.   We only
find out from the administrative practice of the bank
itself.

Sometimes it happens that the bank says, " We do
not pay, the State has released us from our obligation."   Then a bank-note is no longer an effective
promise to pay.   Is it then no longer a bank-note, but
only a piece of paper ?

The incident has happened so frequently in Austria
and other places that there it would be much more
correct to call a bank-note an ineffective means of
payment than an effective one.   But the name bank-
note has continued, and (what is much more important) bank-notes have gone on being used.

We have here only two views to choose between.
Either we must say inconvertible bank-notes are not
bank-notes, though they are so called, or we must say
the above definition of a bank-note [1] has been wrong.

The latter appears to me to be the right conclusion
if we are to be consistent with the general use of
language.   The definition must be altered.   A bank-
note may begin by being an effective promise to pay,
in order to ingratiate itself with the world ; there are
many instances of such cunning in the history of law.

When the bank-note was an effective promise to
pay, it could be used unrestrictedly for making pay-

[1] P. 132 foot.

ments to the bank. If the bank owes me a hundred marks, and I hold one of its notes, I can then certainly use the document, first to get the hundred marks paid out to me, and also secondly to pay the bank a hundred marks if I happen to owe it so much. The note, therefore, is a means of payment to the bank itself. If the bank, in spite of its promise, will not redeem the notes, still the second use continues, the bank accepts the notes in payment.

The fundamental property of a bank-note is, therefore, by no means the promise to pay. A bank-note is a chartal document, which specifies a sum of valuta money; and the bank issuing it is pledged by law to accept it for a payment of that amount. But that is nothing else but a chartal means of payment— issued privately; it is a private till-warrant available for payments to the bank (*epitrapezic payments*). Whether it is also available epicentrically may be left undiscussed; but clearly the customers of the bank can use it for payments between themselves, as they are sure it will be taken at the bank. These customers and the bank form, so to speak, a private pay community; the public pay community is the State.

An inconvertible bank-note, then, is not a nullity, but has this in common with the convertible bank-note, that it is a till-warrant of the bank.

The notion of the note as a till-warrant is not complete until the institution which has the obligation to accept it in payment is named. A bank-note should be defined as a till-warrant of this or that bank. A bank-note can certainly be a bank-note and a Treasury warrant at the same time, but this is not essential.

The question whether the bank-notes form part of the currency can now be answered in a few words. Bank-notes are not automatically money of the State, but they become so as soon as the State announces that it will receive them in epicentric payments. By virtue of this "acceptation," bank-notes become State currency, but only in the wide meaning of the word. Whether they become accessory money or valuta is not yet determined.

Besides, in all circumstances, bank-notes have a remarkable but little noticed property, completely analogous to money of the State. When money of the State is applied in epicentric payments to the State, then it makes absolutely no difference whether valuta or accessory pieces are chosen; for all these pieces have in common the property of being unconditionally received by the State.

Consequently in epicentric payments the question which sort of money is now valuta does not arise, it is a matter of complete indifference and only becomes of interest when the payments are anepicentric payments.

Something similar makes its appearance when bank-notes are used for payment to the bank (epitrapezic payments in bank-notes). Here the question " What sort of money is for the time being valuta ? " is irrelevant. For the bank is under an obligation to receive these notes as so many units of what happens to be valuta money at the time.

But it is another matter if at the same time the bank-note is a promise to pay, for then in the last resort it must be redeemed in valuta money, and the question, of course, arises, " Which sort is now valuta ? "

That bank-notes should make their first appearance as promises to pay is practically necessary, otherwise they would not make their way at all, but this property can be dropped without the bank-notes stopping, as has been seen on innumerable occasions.

Even if the bank stops and settles its obligations, or goes into liquidation, it has to redeem its notes, and that in valuta money, only if they are promises to pay. But if the State has declared them inconvertible and elevated them to the position of valuta notes, then redemption in valuta money is a meaningless expression, because the bank-notes are already valuta. However, the liquidation of a bank during a period when its notes were valuta is unheard of as yet.

It is a great favour to the banking world that the State permits the issue of notes. As is well known, other business men may not issue notes, or private till-warrants. Certainly the State also controls the business by law, for it rightly counts it of public utility. But it is nevertheless remarkable that the profits which are increased by this means, of a magnitude only explainable by the note issue, should flow exclusively to the owners of the capital. The State is giving to the holders of bank shares a means of increasing their profits which it absolutely denies to other businesses. " Capitalism " is thus not indeed begotten but certainly brought up by the State.

Very frequently (almost as a rule) among these banks one is formed which the State supports even more strongly; it makes no contribution to it in money, but announces administratively that the notes of such and such a bank will be received in payment by the State; that is State " acceptation."

For the bank, this means an enormous increase in its profits, for now everybody is glad to take its bank-notes, since all the inhabitants of the State have occasion to make epicentric payments (*e. g.* for taxes). Hitherto it was only the customers of the bank who cared to use this means of payment. But now the circle of users is indefinitely enlarged. So that the State has again increased the business of such a bank, and by a new method. It has announced, " I recognise bank-notes made by you as State pay-warrants."

From that moment these bank-notes become part of the State monetary system and remain there until the State withdraws its recognition. Very often, but not invariably, the State imposes the condition that these notes shall be convertible at the bank; yet sometimes the bank-notes continue to be State pay-warrants after they have ceased to be convertible.

They attain this position not by being convertible, but simply by being recognised by the State.

But being admitted into the State currency means merely being admitted into the currency in the broader sense of the term.   Are they accessory or valuta ? As a rule they are first of all received as accessory money, that is, the State recognises them for epicentric payments, yet when it makes its own payments (apocentric payments) it declares them not to be a final means of payment.   But sometimes the other course is taken, and the State proclaims the bank-notes to be valuta money, so that it can properly make apocentric payments in bank-notes.   This new phase of the bank-note as currency causes much more lively sensation than the other; it is the case first thought of; the former case is easily forgotten, because people are not accustomed to distinguish money from valuta as we do.   It is therefore necessary to lay emphasis on the fact, that if bank-notes become recognised even as accessory money of the State, they have made their appearance as State money.   Elevation to the position of valuta money carries the matter further, but it need not happen.   The notes of our Reichsbank (in 1905), for example, formed part of the currency, but they were only accessory, not valuta money.   In Austria, on the other hand, the notes of the bank have for a very long time been valuta, and they are valuta until they become convertible.

This makes it appear as if we greatly underrated

the importance of the convertibility of the bank-notes, while all economists quite properly attach the greatest importance to it. But our business here is only to show how bank-notes make their appearance as part of the currency, whether convertible or not.

The significance of convertibility has quite a different place in the discussion. Convertibility is first of all important for the bank itself. On the strength of it the bank-notes can be put into circulation without dispute, because every holder has the possibility of obtaining possession of valuta money issued by the State.

But convertibility is also important for the State, after it has recognised the bank-notes as currency, even as accessory money. For so long as the bank is obliged to redeem its notes in money issued by the State, the State does not need to take any further steps in order to keep the bank-notes in their accessory position. The bank looks after that. Convertible bank-notes when they have become part of the currency are already automatically in the subordinate position which we call accessory. They are not a final means of payment for the creditor, because he can demand conversion. The State wants convertibility for the bank-notes since and so long as it allows them to be accessory money. Every State takes care that the notes shall be convertible, and makes this a condition of allowing the bank to have a note issue.

The convertibility of the bank-notes is then one

of the measures by means of which the State assures
a superior position to the money which it issues itself,
certainly a very important object.

According to the general opinion, conversion always
means conversion in specie money; this is another
instance showing how little sense exists for general
theory.

Specie money, as we know, means orthotypic-
hylogenic money. A person who begins to write
about bank-notes cannot help thinking first that there
is that kind of money in the State, and secondly that
it occupies the position of valuta. Now it is certainly
true that there was specie money in all the places
where bank-notes began to be introduced. But it is
not true that specie money is valuta in all the places
where bank-notes are ever in use. We have only to
think of England at the time of the revolutionary
wars, France at the time of the 1870 war, Austria at
almost all times. The contrast to bank-notes is not
specie money as such, but the money issued by the
State, and this may or may not be specie money.
Bank-notes may be convertible in specie money, but
all that is essential is that they should be convertible
in State-issued money, and indeed in valuta.

When convertibility exists, the bank has to give out
against its notes the same amount in State-issued
valuta money. On the other hand, in its own interest
the bank will never refuse to accept State-issued money
and to give in exchange the same sum in bank-notes.

If the bank-notes are convertible there exists a rate of exchange with the State-issued money, which reminds us of hylodromy; but a fixed price is not assured to a definite metal, as in the case of hylodromy. What is assured is a fixed rate for the bank-notes in terms of the State-issued money. No doubt both are determined by an act of the administration.

As a rule this escapes observation the more readily because if the bank-notes are inconvertible they quickly vanish from circulation, unless the State comes to their help with compulsion. All the same it is true that bank-notes get their fixed rate in State-issued money only by a twofold act of the administration—the act making the bank-notes inconvertible in State-issued money and the act making the State-issued money convertible into bank-notes.

It might be expected that the State would always give a preference to the money issued by itself and keep the bank-notes in an accessory position, once they have been received into the State currency at all. The business of the bank would be powerfully furthered, and whoever preferred bank-notes could make use of them if he liked. All concerned would be helped and this state of affairs could continue to the general satisfaction, if sometimes the necessities of the State did not bring about quite another development.

The wide development of the Lombard and Discount business very soon creates for the bank a fortune which greatly exceeds those of private individuals.

In view of the convertibility of the notes, the bank, with or without compulsion, holds a stout store of specie.

The partly passive and partly active help given to the banks is remembered by the State in certain moments of difficulty, especially at the outbreak of war, and still more at the approach of defeat. Its need for money is at the highest pitch; it cannot raise enough by taxes; loans are made very difficult for it or are refused. Then it thinks of the bank which has become great through its help. One good turn deserves another. The bank is scarcely in a position to refuse assistance to its too powerful patron and benefactor, although it is not part of its proper business to grant loans of that sort. Before anyone is aware of it the bank (for example, in Austria) has lent the State 80,000,000 gulden, perhaps on the security of real property (which is quite irregular) or on other security. Certainly in doing so the bank has overstepped the limits prescribed for its business, but its guardian, the State, has compelled it.

Now, if the bank cannot make a corresponding increase in its stock of specie, the bank-notes cannot henceforth be converted. The State understands that very well. It first makes an order and then later a law, that the bank is released from the obligation to convert.

The State takes a further step when it announces " I too do not redeem these notes in specie, because I have not enough specie money; I, the State, shall in future make final payments in the inconvertible bank-notes. I declare these notes to be valuta money. But since my Courts cannot compel my subjects to pay in other ways than those in which I, the State, make payment, these notes are legal tender for all payments among private persons."

By means of this highly remarkable transaction, usually deemed a crushing misfortune for the State, the calm observer makes certain discoveries. Money transactions do not stop; but the valuta money has become something different; it is no longer made out of metal but out of paper. No metallist has ever explained this. He simply decries as anomalous a proceeding often occurring for decades together. Where in the world does any other science allow itself to call any notorious fact anomalous merely because it contradicts the ruling theory? The anomaly is only in the metallistic theory of money; for the Chartal theory there is here nothing remarkable, but only the simplest case of Chartalism. We could almost say that we were glad that at last non-metallic money had come on the scene, the possibility of it having been long in our mind. Common-sense may make us regret the political situation, which brought about such an occurrence, and regret the momentous effects on trade. These emotions do credit to the heart of the public man; but the theorist's business is to explain the facts, without emotion.

It is considered a bad thing that money is now paper pieces. "All money?" you say. No, a great deal of the money. But before this a great deal of money was paper pieces. The magnitude of the change does not consist in the fact that there is no longer any metallic money as part of the currency, but that paper money and metallic money, both as before existing side by side, have interchanged their functional position. That certainly is intelligible only if the antithesis between valuta and accessory money is recognised, as our economists and jurists have hitherto not recognised it. Before the great change the specie money was valuta and the (notal) paper money accessory. After the change the paper money is valuta, and the specie money has become accessory.

This is the point at which the Chartal theory most clearly differs from the Metallist theory.

To the metallist, specie money always remains the chief kind, perhaps at first in the background, but secretly still exerting influence.

This is just what the Chartalist denies. He says, "It is true that the specie money, which before was valuta, is still extant, that is to say, the pieces still exist; but so far as valuta is concerned, they are out of the game. The notes are now the genuine valuta money, not supported by anything. Theory deals with what is; politics can deal with what ought to be."

§ 8b. *Giro or Transfer Payment.*

According to our conception, so long as bank-notes are not State-accepted they form the Chartal money of a pay-society or group which is not the State, and so are a special case of a privately issued means of payment. They have in common with the Chartal money of a State the fact that the payment is in " pieces," a " thing " is delivered; no doubt a thing with a Chartal constitution still is a " thing." It is otherwise with Giro payment. In the first place it is allied to payment in bank-notes in that it occurs in a pay-society which is not the State. The State is not accustomed to organise any Giro payment, although the banks do it frequently.

On the other hand, it differs from payment in bank-notes, because no " pieces " are employed in it. Chartality is excluded here by the absence of the pieces to which Chartality is legally attached.

The essential features of this new phenomenon will first be described in connection with the former Giro [1] bank at Hamburg.

In 1619 the Hamburg merchants founded an institution called the Giro bank, with the object of adjusting mutual payments. Each member delivered

---

[1] See Ernst Levy von Halle, *The Hamburg Giro Bank and what it came to* (Berlin 1891).

L

a certain quantity of silver bullion. Coins were received by the institution not as possessing any Chartal rights, but only as pieces of a known fineness and a given weight. The institution kept the deposited silver in its actual *corpus*, without employing it in any kind of business, and only gave it back when the member demanded it, and so far as he, the depositor, had not himself already infringed on it, the deposit being an interchangeable thing, *res fungibilis*, namely, silver.

The institution now created a unit of value called mark banco, in which it reckoned; *e.g.* for each pound (500 grammes) of the silver delivered, $59\frac{1}{3}$ marks banco were placed to the credit of the depositor (1868).

The mark banco was neither a coin nor a note nor a " piece," but it was the unit in which the amount of the deposit was expressed. A person had a mark banco, who on account of the silver deposited by him had to his credit 1 divided by $59\frac{1}{3}$ pounds of silver. The idea of the arrangement was that members paid one another by ordering the bank to debit the Conto (account) of the payer and credit the Conto of the receiver with so many marks banco—that is, so many units of the deposit. These orders were given in writing, and had to contain the names of both the debtor and the creditor. The creditor was notified by the bank of what had been transferred to his Conto. This is an example of Giro payment in its purest form, transfer of credit from one depositor to another, the means of payment being then only in the legal sense personal property, and there being no transfer of " things."

This is a new hylogenic means of payment. Silver being the *hyle*, the deposit can only be made by the delivery of silver. If gold were to be delivered, then gold would be the hyle for this lytric form.

But this form is not autometallistic. The payment is not a transfer of silver by weight. Weighing is only used when the silver is delivered in at first and when it is delivered out on the withdrawal of the Conto. The deliveries are pensatory; but the payments made through the institution are not pensatory, nor are they chartal; they are a mere matter of transfer; and that is just the meaning of " Giro " payment.

Sometimes it is thought that this Giro payment acts in the same way as silver autometallism, even if externally they differ greatly. But silver kept in the cellars of the bank, and used as the foundation of the members' credit, is more than mere silver; it is changed from the legal point of view, just as gold coined into ducats is by no means the same thing as gold out of which ducats can be coined.

In silver autometallism each pound of silver must *ex definitione* have a fixed price. But this is not the case with the argyrogenic Giro system; it can only be attained by hylodromic arrangements. A fixed price of silver could have been called into being *ex institutione*, if anyone who possessed silver was free to

become a member of the Giro society. But we have
not required such a hylolepsy; the circle of Hamburg
merchants is limited. Only the hylophantic arrangement existed. It was then quite possible that a
pound of silver cost less than $59\frac{1}{3}$ marks banco, but
it was not possible that the members of that Giro
group should offer more than $59\frac{1}{3}$ marks banco for a
pound of silver.

The unit called mark banco had absolutely nothing
to do with the unit that formerly was used in Hamburg, when business was done with State money.
For this reason the mark banco had a varying
rate of exchange against the thaler money, then
in use in North Germany, which yet was equally
argyrogenic, for the mark banco was not regulated
hylodromically.

That a unit of value, the mark banco, was independently established at the Hamburg Giro bank,
unconnected with the unit of value for State money,
is a particularly instructive circumstance; each pay-
group can make a unit of value for itself. The State
can do it, because it is a pay-society, not because it
is the State. The State is only the most familiar, the
oldest society of payers; it is not the only one. So
legal organisation of the pay-society creates the unit
of value. This is a great extension of the point of
view from which we started—that the State was
the only pay-society.

More recently Giro transactions have developed

in such a way that a special Giro bank no longer forms their centre, as it formerly did in Hamburg.

Other banks, especially those confined to Lombard and Discount business, have developed in addition a Giro system, quite independently of the issue of notes. This machinery developed somewhat as follows :

People who wish to become members of the Giro group of a bank make a " payment " into the bank, for which the bank opens an account for them. The payment is made in State money, so that, in contrast with the Hamburg arrangement, no special unit of value is created, but the accounts are kept in the units (mark, franc, pound sterling, etc.) which are already in use in the country. " Payment in " does not discharge a debt, but establishes a credit.

The money paid in is not kept separately by the bank as a specific deposit, but is treated as a non-specific deposit, that is to say, the bank recognises itself only as a debtor [1] to the depositor.

If a member of the Giro association wishes to make a payment to another member, he does this just in the same way as in the Hamburg institution; the bank receives a written order to debit the amount against the deposit of the one and credit it to the deposit of the other.

Since the bank opens a Conto for almost anyone who wishes to make a payment in, and on the other

---

[1] In the ordinary sense. See *infra*, p. 151.

hand will repay it on demand and close the Conto, no particular rate of exchange is developed for the unit of value in Giro deposits. Since the bank is not pledged to keep the corpus of the money paid in, it obtains a considerable stock of money, without incurring any risk that it will all be withdrawn at one time. Thus the working capital of the bank is increased and a great part can be used in businesses which are quite safe and can be terminated at short notice. In this way the bank increases the total of its profits, while the profits are set down only to its paid-up capital. This is why the bank can afford to dispense with a charge in respect of the Giro Conto,[1] and may even pay a little interest to the customers.

One often hears it said that Giro business " saves money." It certainly enables the bank to extend its business further than would have been possible with its original working capital alone. But no money is " saved " for the Giro customer; he is only saved the trouble of carrying money about with him.

There is no counterpart in the Giro business to inconvertibility of bank-notes. The bank is never released from its duty of repaying the deposits of the Giro customers, and it is always bound to allow its own claims against the customers to be satisfied by drafts on the customer's Giro deposits. The analogy would be not that the Giro deposit should be lost, but

[1] Current account is perhaps the nearest English equivalent.—TR.

that it should have ceased to be liquid, but still remain a claim against the bank. This has never been known to occur.

But the Giro customer is by no means assured that on closing his account he will get his money back again in the form in which he has paid it in. He gets back for certain an equivalent amount. But from the bank's point of view his deposit is a lytric debt and therefore measured in units of value. What is paid back will, then, not be the money which was paid in, but the money equivalent to the money paid in. If, meanwhile, the currency of the State has not altered, the repayment will be made in the same money as that paid in. But if in the meantime the currency has altered, the customer must submit to this alteration whether he likes it or not. He is in exactly the same position as all other lytric creditors.

This makes a great difference between the Hamburg Giro and the present. The Hamburg Giro had an independent standard, not connected with the State. Our Giro groups of to-day have the State standard. Another difference which has already been pointed out is that in Hamburg the consignment was of a specific deposit; but, as is well known, in the Giro business of to-day the money paid in only gives rise to a lytric claim against the bank. The resemblance is that both are systems of transfer.

Our survey of Giro business shows us that there is

such a thing as payment without an actual delivery of a thing, so that we must conceive payment in a new way. If the notion of payment is to include both the payment with pieces of money and also the Giro payment, the delivery of " things " cannot be an essential attribute of payment. The essential characteristic of all payment is patent and evident in Giro payment, but must exist latent in payment with pieces.

Payment is a transaction which in any case implies a society, whether it be the State or the customers of a bank or any other kind of association of payers. It might even extend beyond the State, as, in the case of autometallism, it is all those persons who recognise silver, copper, or gold as an exchange commodity.

But when autometallism is gone, the financial group must have administrative guidance; there must be authorities with legal powers to fix the nature and manner of the payment. It must have a centre from which it is managed. In the case of State money, this means the authority of the State; in the case of private methods of payment, it means, for example, a bank.

Payment then in its more comprehensive definition does not require the actual delivery of pieces, but a legal transfer of claims and counter-claims in units of value directed to a Central (Clearing) Office. Such transfer may or may not be made by means of actual delivery of Chartal pieces, that is, of money; Giro payment is not made by the actual delivery of pieces but by means of book entries.

The members of an association of payers make their payments to one another in the following way; Member A delivers a claim which stands to his credit at the central office to member B. By this means the payment is carried out.

We may express the needful co-operation of the central office by saying that the payments are always *metacentric*. It is evident that Giro payment is always metacentric; but so also is Chartal payment, for it is always made in the kind of pieces which are "accepted" by the central office, that is to say, recognised as valid for satisfying claims of the central office. Even pensatory payment is made in this manner, for (when it is a question of payment to the central office) it is always allowable to weigh out the metal used for payment. Hence metacentric payment is a phenomenon common to all associations of payers, while actual delivery, whether of metal or of a Chartal piece, is not.

This enlarges our notion of means of payment. We already know the pensatory and the chartal, and now we have the Giral. All these kinds allow the transfer of claims on the central office, but only the first two kinds perform this transfer by the actual delivery of "things."

But a small difficulty still remains. If I pay in

a pensatory or a Chartal manner, is this the transfer of a claim on the central office?

When the Chartal piece is convertible (*i. e.* provisional), then obviously a claim on the central office is transferred. But if the payment is pensatory, or is made in definitive money, is a claim on the central office also transferred? Obviously not, if we assume the claim to be substantiated and unconditionally payable. A person who holds definitive money (just as the holder of the material for payment in a pensatory system) has no claim on the central office, no unconditionally payable, self-subsistent, absolute claim.

But the notion of a claim can be widened, and we have already tacitly widened it. There are also claims on the central office which only arise when certain conditions are fulfilled, namely, when a debt to the central office has fallen due.

Each definitive means of payment establishes for the holder a claim on the central office which only arises in such event; the holder, at the moment when the central office makes a claim on him—but not before or afterwards—has a counter-claim which he brings to light by the delivery of definitive means of payment for the purpose of discharging his debt. This notion of an eventual counter-claim is lacking in our jurisprudence, while the concept of an absolute counter-claim is quite familiar.

The jurist never refers to an eventual counter-

claim. But why should not this concept be introduced ? By introducing it we can state the case as
follows :

The liquidation of a lytric claim of the central
office is always carried out by means of a set-off, that
is, by bringing a counter-claim into account—either an
absolute one, if at the moment there is one ready, or,
if there is no absolute counter-claim in existence,
by a counter-claim which is only eventual, and that
is always possessed by a person who holds a definitive
means of payment.

By this means the concept " means of payment "
can be defined. In a pay-group every transferable
right to dispose of units of value is a means of payment, if the holder can by transfer set up in the
central office a counter-claim which is at any rate
eventual.

Thereby every material content has vanished from
the concept of means of payment; similarly the
concept of a movable thing is no longer there; that is
to say, neither is essential, so that even a Giro deposit
is included among possible means of payment.

As bank-notes are private money till the State
" accepts " them, so Giro payment, to begin with,
according to its historical origin, is a private payment, but it can also be elevated by " acceptation ";
if the State becomes a member of the Giro community
and allows payments made to it through the Giro
machinery. What is thus " accepted " is not a

" real " means of payment, but a legal method of payment.

If the State managed the Giro machinery in its own name (instead of, as now, leaving it to the banks), then at first this would be only permissive, and would not put an end to payments in State pieces. The Giro method is inconvenient for small payments; Giro payment implies a notice to the managing office, that is, a written order, while payment in pieces of money is a transfer made on the spot where the obligation arises, as in a purchase at the market or booking a railway ticket. Similarly the question may be raised whether, at any rate in theory, the whole business of payment might not be conceived as a State Giro business, so that payment in pieces would be completely abolished. Certainly money would be abolished, but paying would remain. The structure of our economy, which we like to designate a money economy, does not depend on money; it only appears to depend on it because we almost always make our payments by the transfer of money. But that is only a special case. The essential feature is obligations measured in units of value. These would not be abolished with the abolition of money, but retained and managed in the Giro method.

Giro payment, then, completes the system of kinds of payment which stands now as follows :

1. Autometallism (more generally, authylism) where the notion of money has not yet been reached.

2. Chartal payment, meaning the same thing as payment in money, however the kinds of money are further classified.

3. Giro payment, payment without money.

But all this applies to State pay-groups only so far as the State has declared that the above kinds of money are allowed for epicentric payments. This is not the case with all bank-notes, nor is it with all Giro systems, though it is with many of them.

As we said at the beginning of this book, the whole world of payments is a creation of the law; to this we now add the words " of the law in State or private pay-societies." Shortly stated, this proposition runs : The world of payments is a phenomenon of the administration. The administrative phenomenon, which we call payment, is most intimately bound up with the concept of the unit of value which has developed in societies, and cannot be thought of without this concept; but it is quite possible to have a world of payment without authylism, without hylogenic money, even without autogenic money or any money at all. Business payments, however, are not possible without some arrangement for transferring units of value; and Giro business seems to be the final conceivable form of it.

§ 9. *Agio on Accessory Money*

When it is argued that money is not a commodity, because it is itself always a means of payment, the tacit assumption is made—(1) that there is only one kind of money, and (2) that we are dealing only with trade inside the country.

We cannot assume that there is only one kind of money. In all modern States there are many kinds, side by side.

Among the different kinds of money there is always one, which we have called valuta, depending on function and independent of material. The other kinds are called accessory.

The matter stands thus: all obligations expressed simply in money refer in the last resort to valuta, because judicial decision is final and the State as fountain of law only compels obligations to be performed in the money in which it itself (by its Treasury) makes payments.

For this reason it is always valuta money which is contrasted with commodities; inside the country it is never itself a commodity.

So that it is not money simply which is contrasted with the concept commodity, but only valuta money; for *ex definitione* it is only valuta money which is never purchased. But there is absolutely no difficulty in conceiving that accessory kinds of money are purchased; so that they are commodities, even in internal trade.

It is true that accessory money will not be a commodity if the State will exchange valuta money for it when it thinks it advisable to do so.

For this reason the German thalers, in spite of their accessory position, were not commodities. There was no need to buy them, for they could be obtained in voluntary exchange. Not till a very high price of silver returned would it be necessary to buy them. German Treasury notes, too, which were equally accessory, did not need to be bought, because the State was glad to offer them in exchange for our gold money, which was the only valuta.

But there are accessory kinds of money which the State does not offer in exchange for valuta money. From 1859 the Austrian silver gulden was accessory money, but was not paid out by the State in exchange for the valuta notes. No doubt it was still a State means of payment, but in spite of that it could be a commodity. The holder had the choice; he could— like a fool—use the silver gulden for paying; or he could—like a wise man—sell it like any other commodity.

A profit from the sale of an accessory piece of money (within the country) arises only from the possibility of selling such a piece as a material commodity. Whether or not this is profitable depends on the price. The profit on such a piece is called *agio*.

Agio is inconceivable if, as was the case in former ages, there was only one kind of money in a country. It is absolutely necessary to have some other money to compare it with.

Further, agio is inconceivable in the case of valuta

money. This kind of money always behaves as if it were the only one. The agio is, so to speak, measured in degrees from the zero point given by the valuta money. It exists only in comparison with valuta money, so that the latter (within the country) cannot itself have a positive agio.

The agio is particularly striking when the valuta money is made out of paper pieces, and some people think this is the only case. But the agio does not come from the fact that valuta is paper. Accessory kinds of money can have an agio when the valuta is still specie money; and the valuta money may be made of paper, without any agio arising.

Here once again it appears how much the judgment of the theorist differs from that of the practical man.

The use of paper has nothing to do with the question. All that is necessary is that there should be accessory kinds of money by the side of the valuta. If, then, it is more profitable to sell one of the accessory kinds than to put it to a lytric use, then that kind has an agio.

Agio, then, is: the price of an accessory piece of money, treated as a commodity, expressed in the units of value of the country (and payable in valuta money) minus the face value of the piece.

We have treated this difference of value as positive; then it is called Agio; if it is negative, it will be called *Disagio*.

A negative agio (or disagio) implies that an accessory piece of money is treated as a commodity, even at a loss, that it is sold as if it were nothing but a disc of metal, so that the lytric use of it is voluntarily given up. But people do not give it up when they lose by that; so that in practice the negative agio is not in evidence, at any rate for ordinary business. It is only a conceivable case. The State takes notice of it only when it has such accessory pieces in its coffers and for any reason wants to use these platically as metal discs.

In the same way the holder of accessory pieces with a positive agio, if he acts for his own advantage, always uses them platically as commodities, and never lytrically as means of payment. From the legal point of view they still, it is true, remain means of payment, so long as the State makes no alteration in the legal regulations, but in point of fact they cease to be used as means of payment.

On the other hand, accessory pieces with negative agio (disagio) are (so long as the holder acts for his own advantage) always used in a lytric and never in a platic manner, and they continue to be used for business payments. Everybody prefers to pay with these pieces, although he could have paid with other accessory pieces which have a positive agio. This is the real meaning of Gresham's law : " Bad money drives out good." Here by " bad money " is to be understood accessory money with a negative agio,

M

and by " good money," on the other hand, that kind
of accessory money of which the agio is nil, or else
a positive quantity. Understood in this sense, the
Gresham proposition is true; it belongs to the
numerous class of half-truths. But the proposition
relates only to the mutual relations of different kinds
of accessory money.

It is not true when applied to valuta money. If
" good " money is taken to mean specie valuta
money, and " bad " money notal valuta money
(*e. g.* made of paper), then the proposition is quite
absurd. It does certainly occur that notal valuta
money takes the place of the former specie valuta
money (*e. g.* if bank-notes or State notes are made
valuta). But this is not due to the economic
action of holders, looking to their own profit, but to
the action of the State, when its financial strength
is feeble and it decides to treat a notal kind of money
(*e. g.* paper) as valuta and to bring the specie money
which had formerly been valuta into the position of
accessory. That has not come to pass automatically,
nor through the action of the citizens, nor through
the holder considering whether it is more profitable
to use the money lytrically or platically. It has
come to pass through a decision of the State, forced
on it by necessity. As long as the State does not
change its decision, of leaving the formerly valuta
" good " money still valuta, the " bad " money never
drives out the " good."

Which kind of money is valuta always depends on the State, or, to be more precise, on the way it regulates its apocentric ultimate payments.

But which kind of accessory money remains in lytric use depends, of course, on the individuals. Only those kinds of accessory money of which the agio is nil or negative in fact remain in use as means of payment.

We see then that all kinds of accessory money have agio in the wider sense of the word—sometimes positive, at other times negative—and they have the agio nil only in the moments of equilibrium—that is, when the positive agio is changing over into a negative one or *vice versa*. It may happen that all the accessory kinds of money have a positive agio (as for a time in Austria, when not only the silver gulden, but also the small coins, had agio). Or it may happen that all accessory kinds of money have a negative agio (as in Germany since about 1876). Or it may happen that certain kinds of accessory money have a positive and others a negative agio (as in Italy, where the gold twenty-lire pieces had a positive and the silver lire pieces a negative agio). In Germany the thalers, which, as is well known, are accessory, would have had the agio nil if the price of silver had remained at the level of the year 1871. The examples we have cited, so far as they are taken from Germany, show that the notion of agio is in no way connected with the existence of valuta paper

money. We might even live to see the thaler pieces
have a positive agio—if, as is improbable, the price of
silver should rise higher than in 1871 ! Then our State
pay offices would be careful not to offer (still less to
press upon us) thalers in apocentric payments, although
they could do so in 1905 as the law then stood.

Accessory kinds of money with a positive agio are
no disadvantage to the holder; they are even an
advantage, since he makes a profit on selling them.
But, for the monetary system as a whole, the result
is that such money is withdrawn from lytric use.
In this way a positive agio can produce great embarrassment, for example, if it occurs in the indispensable pieces of low denomination, *e. g.* the silver
one- or two-franc pieces (France, 1865). The pieces
with a negative agio are then diligently turned out
with a reduced fineness of metallic content. As the
amount of fine metal has nothing to do with the
validity, this proceeding puzzles only the metallist,
who regrets to see that for the public benefit a
transition has been made to pieces of negative agio.

Accessory kinds of money with a positive agio, if
their discs are used as a commodity, are worth more
lytric units than they are valued in as means of
payment; "to have value" (in exchange) is a
property of commodities, to have validity is a legal
property of Chartal pieces. For this reason we may
say that accessory money with a positive agio is
appreciated or over-valued, and, analogously, acces-

sory money with a negative agio we can call depreciated, or under-valued; if the accessory money
happens to have the agio nil, then it can be called
full-valued.

The terms over-valued and under-valued have
absolutely no meaning in regard to valuta, because
valuta money is not used as a commodity. It must
not be forgotten that the concept value always
requires a comparison of terms. No doubt the
terms can be chosen by arrangement. Nobody can
prevent us from comparing the commodity wheat
with the commodity oats, and saying that a bushel
of wheat is worth so many bushels of oats. But
" value " *sans phrase* means the value of a commodity
in terms of money; and, if there is more than one
kind of money in the country, the value in valuta
money is always meant.

The question can certainly be asked, " What is the
value of valuta money in terms of silver, gold, corn
or petroleum ? " but in this case the thing with which
it is to be compared is expressly stated. We shall
not deal with this question, nor shall we assume that
any particular metal has a fixed price in terms of
valuta money. From our point of view it is at this
point a matter of complete indifference whether there
is metallodromic control or not. Our concern is with
that money which according to the rule and ordinances
in force can be demonstrated to be valuta.

Appreciation and depreciation of accessory money

(or, what is the same thing, positive or negative agio) mean, then, a certain relation to the valuta money for the time being; there is no idea of comparison with any metal. Our concept of valuta money is a functional one; and metallodromy is not essential for valuta.

The phenomenon of agio is then formulated in such a manner as to hold good, whether the metal is used platically or not, and also whether it is regulated dromically or not.

From this point of view it is, for example, absolutely clear and logically correct to say that after 1879 the Austrian silver gulden had a negative agio; it was depreciated in relation to the valuta money, which at that time consisted of paper notes. We do not ask which of the two pieces had the greater value if it was sold as mere material, but whether a silver gulden-piece was worth as much as a gulden in notes; and it was worth less.

If anyone cares to ask which of the kinds of money contained the greater quantity of silver, he will certainly get the reply, silver gulden. But that is not the point. A silver gulden considered as a commodity can also in our sense be depreciated (have a negative agio), while, considered as a means of payment, it is worth just as much as a paper gulden.

That the silver gulden was once valuta (1858) and that many people would be glad to see it reinstated is a matter of legal history and lytric policy with which we are not concerned. Dethroned kings are kings no longer.

The agio of accessory kinds of money, be it positive or negative, is a mercantile phenomenon, and so incessantly changes according to the state of the market. It is not then surprising if the agio which in 1903 attached to our thalers was at one time greater, at another time less, according as the price of the metal silver, which is not subjected to our regulations, was lower or higher. Admittedly this agio is latent, because nobody is such a fool as to sell a thaler as a commodity; but it is there notwithstanding. If the price of silver should rise again to the height it was in 1871, the negative agio would cease, without having affected even the least important of our monetary regulations.

Similarly, the height of the positive agio of accessory kinds of money depends only on the conditions of the market. Thus it can at times diminish, vanish, and even become negative without any rule of the monetary system being affected. A positive agio only arises if it is possible to use the pieces profitably as commodities; it vanishes as soon as they can no longer be put to such a use. This too is seen instinctively as long as the monetary system is " normal," that is, so long as specie money is valuta.

If, *e. g.*, in France the silver money had been treated as valuta (from 1803 to about 1860) the gold pieces would now and then have had a positive agio. After 1860 the positive agio vanished because gold in the French market fell in price. But at first there was no change in the French monetary system. One day the positive agio had ceased to exist, and this would only seem remarkable to those people who cherished the superstition that gold had a fixed price in terms of valuta silver money. To all others it was quite plain that the conditions of the market for gold were the cause of the disappearance of the positive agio.

When in Austria in 1878 the positive agio of the silver gulden (which had existed till then) vanished, people thought that something strange had happened. Yet the occurrence was completely analogous. In the market for silver it was no longer profitable to dispose of silver gulden as commodities. For the Austrian market for silver the price of silver meant the price in valuta money, as it always does, but at that time the notes were valuta. Those who decried the note system thought the notes were really an order for silver gulden; they did not see the completely independent nature of this means of payment. But for us who know that the notes were really valuta, it is perfectly comprehensible that the accessory silver gulden should have lost their positive agio, and after 1879 in Austria the silver gulden, which remained accessory, maintained a negative agio with reference to the notes. Why not, if silver

fell still further in price ?   The price of silver expressed
in paper gulden, which at that time were valuta, was
no subject of regulation.   There was no fixed price
of silver in terms of notes.   The price of a silver
gulden could stand above or below, or by chance
for a short time be equal to a gulden note.   Before
1879 it was above, after 1879 below.   The prices of
all commodities are in valuta money; when notes
are valuta, they have nothing more to do with the
money which formerly was valuta, but now (like the
silver gulden since 1859) has become accessory.

The vanishing of the positive agio of the silver
gulden in 1879 and the occurrence of the (invisible)
negative agio after 1879 are simply the consequences
of the fall in the price of silver on the Austrian
market, to be considered by and by.

Up to 1879 the coinage of silver into gulden was
quite free, but after 1879 it was stopped.   The
stoppage of free coinage had nothing whatever to do
with the fact that after 1879 the silver gulden were
treated in business just as the notes were.   The notes
then continued to be valuta, and the silver gulden
came back into lytric business as accessory money
only because, owing to the low price of silver, it had
a negative agio.   The closing of the mint had nothing
to do with the validity.   For the silver gulden had
not the validity of a gulden because the silver it
contained reached this or that price in the market
measured in valuta money, but because this piece

was proclaimed as the lytric unit, a gulden. A paper gulden has the validity of a gulden for exactly the same reason. Pieces proclaimed to be of the same value circulate side by side, the accessory by the side of the valuta. The accessory only goes out of lytric use if, on account of a positive agio, it becomes a commodity, but if the agio is negative it remains in circulation, whether the agio be large or small.

Accessory kinds of money with a positive agio are, as has been mentioned, the most unsuitable kind of money conceivable, for they leave the lytric circulation and become commodities. This is so evident that the State never intentionally makes such kinds of money. The question is whether the State does or does not wish to retain its valuta money unaltered. If the State does not intend any change to occur in the kind of money which it uses as valuta for its apocentric payments, then in the case of coins used as accessory money a positive agio can be produced only by market changes, that is, by changes in the price of the metal out of which these coins are struck. When, for example, in England the gold guinea was proclaimed to be twenty-one shillings at a time when the English used the silver money as valuta, the guinea can only have had an agio (e. g. been saleable for 21s. 6d. or 22s.) if the price for the commodity gold rose correspondingly, and this price, as we know, has to be reckoned in valuta money, which in the case we are considering is silver money. But this is not the only way in which a positive agio arises, it can also creep in if the State changes the kind of money which is valuta. The metal market still co-operates, but the process works out in a different way. When the change is made to another kind of valuta money, the kind which now has ceased to be valuta and has become accessory is not always abolished, but sometimes is retained in a subordinate position as part of the monetary system. Willy nilly, the meaning of all prices has been changed; though they keep the same names they refer to the new valuta money. This also applies to the price of metals, and so it can easily happen that the money which has ceased to be valuta acquires an agio, because now the price is in terms of the new valuta money. In this way the Austrian silver gulden acquired their positive agio since 1859; thenceforward the price of silver meant its price in notes, for these had become valuta. But the note money had no argyrodromy, and it is in terms of this money that the silver prices rise. So that, without anything particular having happened to silver in the rest of the world, in Austria arose a positive agio for silver gulden. It was sufficient that, on account of the change to another valuta money, the silver prices in Austria were no longer under regulation, and in fact they rose. It was not the silver market, but the altered basis for price quotations, which was to blame for the agio.

We will not inquire here why the price of silver in paper gulden was higher than it was before; we will only observe that in this instance the choice of another valuta money has produced the phenomenon of a positive agio for the silver gulden, which was not the case with the English guinea.

It follows from the nature of the case that kinds of money with a positive agio are not deliberately created, but are only called into being by an alteration in prevailing conditions.

The case is otherwise with accessory kinds of money, which have a negative agio; sometimes they are created deliberately, though sometimes merely through a change of the conditions.

Whenever paper Chartal pieces are introduced in an accessory position we know at the outset that they will have a negative agio. Similarly, on the introduction of coins of small value, struck intentionally with a small, or even without any, content of pure metal, it is known at the outset that they will have a negative agio unless quite special conditions intervene. Lytric policy has no fundamental objection to accessory kinds of money with a negative agio, but may deliberately call them into being.

All the more remarkable is the irritation felt by many theorists, if it happens that an accessory kind of money incurs a negative agio through an undesigned change of circumstances. This occurred to our German thalers, which, owing to the valuta position of our gold pieces and the present much lower price of silver (than in 1871), have a negative agio (in 1905).

According to their origin the thalers were (in 1905) an ex-valuta kind of money; they came down to us from a time in which they once had been valuta, and they have been kept on as accessory money. Their property of being ex-valuta is only an historical incident, which has nothing to do with the Chartal law of the present day.

According to the present state of the law the thalers are only an example of accessory pieces, which the law both did and does recognise as current money and which have obtained a negative agio through the conditions of the silver market.

The only difference between them and other kinds of accessory money with a negative agio is that according to the law in 1905 they were still current money, that might be used for payments to any amount.

For those theorists who judge a monetary system only according to statute law, and not according to the much-farther-reaching administrative law, such a kind of money was, in fact, highly suspicious. For it was possible that one day the State when it made apocentric payments would make a practice of forcing thalers on its creditors, the law allowing it to do this as the thalers retained their property of being current money. Obviously this was a danger, if one adhered to the view that in Germany only the gold pieces ought to be valuta, for the State had the support of the law if it wished to give the thalers the position of valuta; it might make its apocentric payments in thalers, and refuse to convert them, and then this kind of money became valuta.

This state of the law betrays some vacillation and lack of judgment. The State ought to make it clear what kind of money it wishes to keep as valuta, and ought not to concede a position as current money to any other kind of money (in our case the thalers).

But the omission had no results, for our administrative law filled the gap. According to the directions of our authorities, in particular of the Reichsbank, which was entrusted with the Chartal administration, the thalers were on principle not to be forced on anyone, and were accordingly not made valuta. In this way the danger was removed, not by law, but by administration. There was undoubtedly a weakness in the Chartal law of Germany.

On the other hand, there was nothing dubious *per se* in the fact that thalers were an accessory money with a negative agio. Bank-notes and Treasury notes, for example, were so likewise. A thaler in Germany was even in fact (though not in law) convertible, and was merely an instance of a convertible accessory piece with a negative agio; it was a coin of which the functional position resembled that of the German Treasury note, as the property of being current money for apocentric payments had, so to speak, gone to sleep.

Two errors are current about the nature of accessory money.

In Germany (if we suppose ourselves in 1905) all these kinds of money are convertible into valuta money, not all of them by statute, but all of them by administrative direction. The conclusion may be drawn that the accessory kinds of money keep in circulation by the side of the valuta money because they are convertible, that they are effectual drafts on valuta money, that in Germany it is to no one's interest to refuse effectual drafts on gold money; the silver five-mark piece will be accepted for five marks, since a large number of five-mark pieces can always be exchanged at the Reichsbank into a correspondingly small number of gold pieces. Now it cannot be denied that in Germany all accessory moneys have the position of convertible Chartal pieces. But this is not the reason why they circulate by the side of the valuta money and are accepted at their face value. If some fine day the administrative provision, under which the thalers are convertible, was abolished, the thalers would still go on circulating as three-mark pieces, in the same way as the silver five-mark pieces and the copper pfennigs. Even the bank-notes and Treasury bills would continue to be used at their face value, though their convertibility had been abolished, but, of course, only if the State maintains the position that those pieces will be received at public pay-offices at their face value.

The reason why accessory kinds of money maintain themselves in circulation as nominal money is simply the fact that they have been proclaimed as accepted for payments in lytric units to the State pay-office; that is, they depend on a fiat, just as is the case with valuta money. If we imagine the convertibility to lapse, the consequence would be that in making payments to the State pay-offices people would always make use of that kind of accessory money which they did not want to keep.

The accessory kinds of money would therefore arrive at the State pay-offices by the way of payment, as they now do by conversion. This would be very inconvenient for the public, but would not have the least effect on the validity of the pieces, since this is fixed by law.

The other common error is that it is necessary to limit the production of accessory kinds of money (as, for example, thalers or silver coins in Germany) in order that they should maintain their face value. In point of fact the coinage of thalers is stopped; there are definite provisions as to the quantity of Imperial silver coins which may be minted. Many people think that the removal of these limitations would have an influence on the quoted value of these pieces. This too is wrong. If to-day we had free coinage of thalers and also of Imperial silver coins, then, just as before, a thaler would be valued at three marks, and the five-mark piece at five; the only result would be that if convertibility were maintained there would be a great rush to convert them. If the convertibility were abolished, these pieces would be used in preference to others for epicentric payments, so that the State pay-offices would not know what to do with their superfluity of accessory money. This is very embarrassing for the State, but it has no consequences for the quotation of the thaler; that is determined by fiat, not by trade. The case just mentioned came to pass in the United States through a temporary acceptance of silver to be coined into dollar pieces. Also it is not true that the State would have to alter its valuta money; and this did not happen in the States.

§ 10. *The Piling up of Accessory Money*

The standard, in the narrower sense of the word, is that kind of money in which the State makes its apocentric payments. If the State pay-offices are always to be ready to make their payments in valuta money, while the State allows accessory money to be used in payments to it, then it can easily come to pass that the State uses up its store of valuta money. The State must be ready to pay out in this kind of money, while it is not at all certain to get it back when it receives money in payment.

N

Even when the economy of the State is in excellent order, that is to say, when in the course of each year it only expends as much money as it is certain to receive, this danger still remains. What guarantee is there that if the State is willing to receive payments in accessory money, it will always have enough of valuta money in hand?

The stocks of money at the State pay-offices, although they are sufficient according to their face value, may contain an uncomfortably high proportion of accessory to valuta money. The valuta money may flow into its coffers in quantities too small for the payments which the State has to make. The Budget balances; but the State's capacity to pay in valuta money is threatened. Thus there arises the question of the " piling up " of the accessory kinds of money in the coffers of the State and the " vanishing " of the valuta money from them.

We have subdivided accessory kinds of money into those which have a positive agio (appreciated) and those which have a negative agio or disagio (depreciated). The former kind will not be used for payments because it is more profitable to treat them as commodities; they will not be used for payments to the State, consequently they will not be " piled up " in the coffers of the State.

But exactly the opposite takes place with accessory kinds of money of negative agio. To use them as commodities is bad business; they will be used as means of payment, that is, they will only have a lytric use. And since they are certain to be accepted at State pay-offices (or they would not be State money), they can easily be " piled up " there. So the State runs the risk of the accessory kinds of money with negative agio being piled up in its coffers and driving out the valuta money; the State may be no longer able to pay in the money which hitherto had been valuta. The standard, which till then had been maintained, is in danger of collapse. Proceeding to enumerate the measures taken to prevent such a state of affairs, we ask, " Who creates the accessory money with a negative agio ? " that is, " Who gives the impetus which causes new pieces of such a kind of money to be produced ? "

Sometimes it is the State itself, for example, when it produces small money. A negative agio does not form part of the notion of small change; its essential characteristic is that it is only legal tender up to a limited amount. But as a matter of fact small change is made so that, as a rule, it has a negative agio.

Similarly, the State itself sometimes issues notes; as they are impressed worthless pieces of paper, they always have a negative agio; but only so long as they are accessory do they belong to the case which we are now considering.

The State can easily regulate the two kinds of accessory money which have just been mentioned, for it has the issuing of them in its own hands.

The State only produces small change so far as people want it, and easily observes the accessory money piling up in its coffers, beyond its wants. As a rule an amount is "rationed out"; (say ten or fourteen or twenty marks per head of the population). The object of this measure is not (as is frequently believed) to protect the business world from an excess of this kind of money; there cannot be more of it in circulation than is required, because it is legal tender only up to a limited amount for apocentric payments, but to an unlimited amount for epicentric payments. But the object is to avoid the piling up. The case is just the same with notes if the State issue them as accessory money; the permissible amount can easily be fixed by careful experiment; when they begin to pile up, no more are wanted in circulation. Often a definite total is fixed in advance by a rule, as *e. g.* in Germany. But this is "restriction," that is, the maintaining of the issue at an arbitrary amount merely as a measure to prevent the piling up in the State's chests.

The case is not the same with bank-notes when they have been received as accessory State money. Not the State, but a bank issues this kind of money. Either it is under the direction of the State (as is the Reichsbank in Germany), or it is a private bank. But a bank is always considered as an undertaking for profit, even if it is a State-directed bank with official duties. The State prescribes the sphere of business of such banks. It admits the notes of the banks into the State currency only on the condition that they are convertible, which in the last resort means convertible into valuta money. There is no danger that bank-notes, when they have become and continue to be accessory money, will be piled up in the coffers of the State. The State will present for conversion at the place of issue all the pieces it considers superfluous, and will be sure to get valuta money for them. Such notes do not drive the valuta money out of the coffers of the State. Hence the State can, without hesitation, accept the notes of such banks at its own pay-offices; it secures itself against a " piling up " by imposing on the banks the duty to convert. But, if the banks should not be in a position to do this, the watchful State would observe the coming danger and make it known in good time that in future such notes will not be received at the State pay-offices; they would then cease to be State money. It is not essential that the note issues of a bank should be limited. Such limitation is made for greater security; but the convertibility of the notes alone already gives a sufficient security.

In more recent times another kind of accessory money with negative agio has frequently arisen, not through the issue of it, but through delay in calling it in. Such are the thaler in Germany, the five-franc piece in France, the silver gulden in Austria and the silver rouble in Russia.

In all of them the State has changed to a new standard, but has left in circulation as accessory money those kinds of money which were valuta under the former standard. Owing to the altered conditions of the silver market, this ex-valuta money has got a negative agio.

In all of them the ex-valuta money, after it had got a negative agio, was piled up in the State pay-offices, and where there was a State bank it was passed on to this bank. The bank had to take it, not in its commercial capacity, but as agent of the Chartal administration. Thus a stock of accessory money with negative agio was produced not by the deliberate issue of such a kind of money, but by delay in calling in the money, which had become ex-valuta. Some of these pieces of money go into circulation, that is to say, they are used for anepicentric payments. But another part, because it can always be used for epicentric payments, is passed on to the State pay-offices and finally forms " dead stock " in the cellars of the bank or the Treasury. The result is that the State Treasury must pay in valuta, but must endure accessory money with a negative agio as well as valuta money, for its receipts and its stock in hand. This makes it difficult for the State to maintain the standard which it has determined on. It begins to suffer from having taken half-measures. An unforeseen circumstance gets in its way. It suffers from the superstition that any metal money is good enough.

The " dead stocks " ought to be cleared off. But if the State dechartalises such kinds of money, that is, if it removes by law their property of being money, then it has them on its hands, and the sale entails a financial loss because the agio is negative.

This happened in Germany and France. It was not a hopeless system of currency that thereby arose; nor in either of the countries mentioned was the gold standard ruined, for this subsists so long as the State treats the gold pieces alone as valuta. But the proceeding created a dead stock which made it very difficult for the State to maintain its standard; it must accept kinds of money which it has decided in no circumstances to pay out again.

In Austria and Russia the case in one respect was the same. The reappearance of the silver gulden and the silver roubles in circulation, as soon as the agio of these pieces became negative, similarly brought this silver money back into the State pay-offices and disturbed the purity of the paper standard.

The return of a metalloplatic money, even if accessory, was hailed by some with satisfaction; and no further attention was given to the matter, though it might have given much food for reflection.

To prevent the impression being created that it is only silver money which can become a burden on the State pay-offices as accessory money with a negative agio, we will call to mind France at the time when the price of silver was high (about 1860–1870). At that time France had a silver standard. The gold money was accessory and not done away with. But so long as the State continued to treat the silver money as valuta, it was the gold money which formed a dead stock in its coffers and made it difficult to maintain the silver standard. The gold money was then accessory and had a negative agio. Very soon the State changed its policy : it decided to treat the gold money as valuta. Because of this change, the episode, theoretically very instructive, was soon past and over.

Finally, ex-valuta paper money too can continue in an accessory position, after the State has adopted any kind of metal standard. This would, for example, have been the case if Austria in 1892 had determined to retain as accessory money a part of its State notes, say the fifty-gulden ones, while (we will suppose) the gold crown pieces had become valuta. Then such paper money would have had a negative agio. But, in the accessory position which we suppose, it would have formed a kind of money which was always received at the State pay-offices, but yet could not be used apocentrically in all circumstances. It would therefore have been possible that these notes should be piled up in the State pay-offices and to that extent they would in some degree make it difficult to maintain the gold standard.

If then the State wishes to introduce a particular form of standard, it always makes it more difficult to attain its end, if it retains an ex-valuta kind of money as accessory money and if this money then or subsequently acquires a negative agio.

The matter is of no importance for the inhabitants of the country unless the State is compelled to abandon its standard. Then for the first time trade feels the bad effects.

The whole proceeding is due to fiscal parsimony. The State desires a certain standard, but hopes to attain this end at small expense.

In our survey of the ex-valuta money which through its negative agio has become a burden on the State, we have hitherto assumed that it was a matter of the old pieces or, to be more precise, of those which arose during the period of the former standard and have lasted on. The number of such pieces cannot be increased, they are a remnant, the dead branches of a tree.

The matter can become much more serious if accessory money with a negative agio continues to be issued, whether coins or paper.

Suppose that after 1876 we had gone on striking thalers, after the gold coins had become valuta and the price of silver had fallen much lower than it fell in 1871; then we should have intentionally made a further issue of a kind of money with a negative agio. As we know, this did not happen.

In France after 1870 there was at first a paper standard. With the fall in the price of silver which began soon afterwards, the blanks of the silver five-franc pieces were worth less than their legal face-value. Nevertheless the free coinage of silver continued till 1876, that is to say, accessory money with a negative agio went on being issued without any limitation.

In Austria in 1879, when a paper standard was in force, the case was the same. The agio of the silver gulden vanished and became negative; but nevertheless at first the total of silver gulden could be increased (it is true only with silver produced in the State mines); that is, the State allowed the further issue of accessory money with a negative agio.

So during the period of high prices of silver France continued to allow gold pieces to be struck, although at that time accessory money with a negative agio.

Suppose that in Germany we had allowed a further issue of Treasury notes, which, as is known, were restricted to a total of 120 million marks, this would be an issue of accessory money with a negative agio.

States are careful in one case only, the issue of paper money, feeling an innate horror of paper. But when it is a question of issuing metal money with a negative agio they are less fastidious. They share the vulgar belief that metal is less dangerous, and overlook the fact that there may be metal moneys with a negative agio. It is not till the pile has become great that they bestir themselves and think of remedies, either changing the standard or discontinuing the further issue.

The best known instance is the discontinuance of the coinage of silver in France, 1876, and in Austria, 1879.   Here it was not the silver, regarded as a metal, which was to blame, but the persistent issue of accessory money with a negative agio.   Discontinuing the issue means closing the mints, because it is coins that are in question.   The State thus protects itself against a further piling up of this kind of money in its coffers or in those of the bank, acting as a Chartal office.

When the further issue went on, there were two cases to be distinguished according as (*a*) the State alone issued or (*b*) private individuals issued such money.

The first occurred in Austria, where " Aerarian " or Treasury silver, that is, the silver from State mines, was coined into gulden after 1879 in spite of the negative agio.   There are silver gulden dated 1890 which came from this source, and this coining did not stop till 1892.   The Treasury made a so-called coinage profit, coining a cheap material into gulden, when the blanks had a much lower than the face value. The State as Treasury acted against the interests of the State itself, which yet at the same time is the guardian of the standard.   The profit which the State makes as Treasury it loses again later, if it should go over to a gold standard.   Lightly come, lightly go, or, if this loss should not become evident, these pieces subsist as a kind of money with a negative agio and cause the piling up we have so often mentioned.

But it is a still worse business when the issue of accessory kinds of money with a negative agio is in the hands of private persons. This occurred in Austria when free coinage of silver continued, although the State no longer had a silver standard, and in France when free coinage of gold continued, although the State had not yet a gold standard.

Private people buy cheap metal, that is, metal the blanks of which, by the mint standard, cost much less than their value as coins. They deliver this metal to the State to be coined and, by force of the still subsisting law, they compel the State to issue such money. The private individuals pocket the profit. But, now that the money has once been made by the State, it remains a burden on the State; the private individuals enjoy the profit on coining, but the future loss or burden falls on the State.

What would the State say if a maker of hemp paper delivered several hundredweight at the State debt office with a request that it should be turned into Treasury notes which he quietly took home, while the notes remained a liability on the State. Could anything be more crazy?

Let us assume that the paper merchant gives an order to the State for 100,000 francs in Treasury notes, but he is ready to offer 60,000 francs in gold pieces for them, so that his profit (exclusive of the material of the paper) amounts to 40,000 francs. The State would count him mad; but he is only asking what a man who delivers silver actually obtains when the price is low and coinage remains free for private persons. And that happened for years in France and for months in Austria.

This case must not be confused with a permitted issue of bank-notes. Certainly in so far as they are recognised as accessory, they have a negative agio : also the issue is undoubtedly put in the hands of private persons; but the State imposes on the issue the obligation to convert them into valuta money. So the State secures itself against loss and against the risk of a " piling up."

But in the case of the free coinage of accessory money with a negative agio the State forgets this guarantee, it does not impose any further obligation on the issuer, or (more correctly) on the person who occasions the issue. Here the State has not, so to say, the recourse to the author of the issue, while in the case of the bank-notes such a recourse is forthcoming. The private individual in the other case can compel the State to make accessory money with a negative agio, the burden of which falls on the State alone, and the profit on which accrues solely to the private person who gives the order.

To get rid of such a nuisance, our State, in its ignorance of the nature of money, must first make experiments (if the State should ever do that). But,

say the metallists, " Metal is metal "; and so we bring
on the scene the jobbers (*agioteurs*), who are far more
mischievous than the coiners.

Everywhere in Europe such proceedings were soon
stopped. But it was otherwise in the United States
of America. After gold money had become valuta,
private persons interested in silver mines, after the
fall in price, succeeded in compelling the State to
purchase silver and to coin it into dollars of the old
Mint standard. But since the State maintained the
gold money in its valuta position, these silver dollars
were accessory, and owing to the low price of silver
had a negative agio. They were not forced on people
by the State, but they were bound to be received by
the State. The result was that the pieces were piled
in the cellars of the Treasury. The affair could be
explained only by the influence of powerful interests
on legislation, in a type of Government which offers
opportunities to such people. The State might just
as well have been expected to buy petroleum at a
price which was profitable for the producers and to
hoard it up in innumerable casks, carefully laid in
the earth. It is no longer a question of Chartal
policy; the State becomes a tool of powerful parties,
until yet more powerful parties put a stop to the evil.

The above examples are concerned with the right of
private individuals to compel the State to make a
further issue of accessory current money consisting
of coins of the old Mint standard while the price of

the corresponding metal is now so low that the pieces have a negative agio. The newly-issued money is either definitive or convertible into valuta money : it makes no difference whether it is convertible directly or by a roundabout process.

If it is definitive it pushes its way by degrees into the State pay-offices. The holder uses it for epicentric payments only as far as he has the occasion to make such. If the opportunity is wanting he uses this kind of money anepicentrically. Some holder or other will find an opportunity for epicentric use, and after a time that kind of money will be thrust into the coffers of the State, where it can remain lying in a pile, since, as we suppose, the State wishes to persist in its standard and so avoids paying out again this accessory kind of money. This happened with the silver dollars of North America; the same thing happened in France so long as there the accessory metal current money was not convertible directly or indirectly.

But, if the State at the same time treats that kind of accessory current money as convertible, directly or indirectly, into valuta money, then the private person who is able to compel the issue of accessory current money with a negative agio will at the same time have in his hands the means of at once obtaining valuta money for himself, and thus at once extracting this money from the State pay-offices. In such a case the feat above mentioned is accomplished more quickly. This happened in Austria when the free coinage of silver continued after the silver agio had vanished, for silver gulden could be immediately changed at the bank for valuta paper money.

To sum up. We assume that the State possesses a definite form of standard, whether it has introduced this voluntarily or under the stress of circumstances. Under this standard the accessory kinds of money have a positive or a negative agio. With a positive agio they have no significance for the questions before us.

Among monies with a negative agio can be further distinguished the kinds which are convertible into valuta money at a private institution such as a bank; they do not endanger the maintenance of the standard, because the State can insist on the conversion of them.

We are left then with those kinds of accessory money with a negative agio which cannot be converted at a private institution; it matters not whether they are convertible at the State pay-offices or not. These kinds of money threaten to be piled up in the State pay-offices, and undoubtedly endanger the maintenance of the standard which the State desires to maintain. Thus positive agio is correlated with a negative " piling " and negative agio with a positive " piling."

The State takes precautions against the pile by " rationing " certain kinds of money, providing that only a certain amount of such money per head of the population may be in circulation; or else the new further creation of such kinds of money is forbidden; the Mint (as we say) is closed.

If it takes no such measures, the State runs the risk of finding after a time that those kinds of money which it wishes to use as definitive money for its apocentric payments are no longer in its coffers.

But, if the State, as in France, allows the choice of valuta money to be determined by the condition of its coffers, if then it pays in silver money when silver money is pouring in, but in gold money if gold money is pouring in, then it has no fixed policy in relation to the standard, but allows itself to be guided by Treasury interests.

A fixed policy in relation to the standard can only be obtained by taking resolute steps to prevent the piling up of accessory kinds of money.

We are not now judging whether the standard is suitable or not. Assuming any kind of actual standard, we are trying to show that the admission of accessory kinds of money with a negative agio will make the standard extremely difficult to maintain.

The use of accessory money is only objectionable so far as its excessive employment exposes the State to that danger.

When the State changes its standard, it should do so for reasons of policy, and not because of embarrassments due to its own careless management of the accessory money.

o

§ 11. *Changes of Standard*

The change from one kind of valuta money to another can only come by the will of the State, valuta meaning the kind of money with which the State makes its apocentric payments.

When the State, in deciding to make the change, relies on the accumulated stocks of accessory money, the change may be called *obstructional*. When the State ignores any accumulation and pushes the change through by its own strong will without regard to any inconvenience of piled-up stocks, we shall call the change *exactory*.

Further, the State in changing the standard may be re-establishing an old standard; this is a *restoratory* change. If it is an entirely new standard, the change is *novatory*. Finally, the alteration may mean (*a*) a rise or (*b*) a poise or (*c*) a fall.[1]

Suppose that the money which is chosen as the new valuta formerly formed part of the existing currency only as accessory money.

If (1) the money which is to be the new valuta has a positive agio, the alteration means a rise.

If (2) the money which is to be the new valuta has no agio, the change to the new standard means a poise or balance.

If (3) the money which is to be the new valuta has a negative agio, then the movement is a falling one.

---

[1] A going up to something higher, a falling down to something lower, or an equipoise, in pendulous oscillation (*Schwebend*).—Tr.

The new standard is not judged by relation to a metal, but by relation to the old standard, on the supposition that the new money had a place in the old system as accessory money.

The most common change of standard is the obstructional, for it demands no sacrifice from the exchequer, and the State is often unaware of its own action, but thinks it is submitting to an economic necessity. By its toleration of an excess of accessory money the valuta is driven out of the public pay-offices. The State begins to pay in a kind of money which hitherto was accessory. Its Budget may be completely in order, the State not paying out more than it receives. But there is a piling up of accessory money. If then the State raises one of these kinds of accessory money into the position of valuta for definitive apocentric payments, then there has been an *obstructional* change to a new standard.

Perhaps this was how England came to the gold standard. Suppose that after the guinea had been proclaimed a piece of twenty-one shillings, and at first had been treated as accessory, that it at some time acquired a negative agio compared with the then valuta silver money, so that guineas were piled up in the vaults. If then the State had taken to paying in guineas, that would have been an obstructional change.

It is quite certain that this was how France came to a gold standard about 1860. The State became tired of always paying out the valuta silver money and never getting it back, the gold money which then had a negative agio being paid in. There was no bankruptcy of the State, there was merely an alteration in the standard; but it was really a kind of valuta bankruptcy, for the State found that it could not continue to pay in the money which till then had been valuta, unless by such burdensome expedients as silver loans.

A paper standard often arises in just the same way. At first bank-notes and Treasury notes are employed only as accessory money. They have already *per se* a negative agio; they begin to be piled up in the vaults, if they are bank-notes not convertible by the private issuer, or if they are Treasury notes, issued in excess. The mournful hour arrives when the State has to announce that it can no longer pay in the money that was till then valuta and that those warrants themselves are now valuta. In this case everyone talks of the valuta bankruptcy, yet the former case is morphologically exactly the same. The State bows to necessity. French bimetallism even elevates it into a principle that the necessities and not the will of the State shall decide the matter.

On the contrary, in *exactory* changes the State does not follow fiscal convenience and lean on an actual accumulation, but by force of will establishes as valuta a kind of money recognised by it to be suitable.

The exactory change is *restoratory* if the State restores a kind of money into its former position as valuta.

This implies that in the existing currency there is a kind of money which formerly was valuta but now has become accessory and has a positive agio.

The following well-known example will make this clear.

During the Napoleonic wars England fell into a paper standard. When peace was concluded in 1815, preparations were at once made to restore the gold standard, and in a few years this was done. The process was purely restoratory in spite of the fact that the guinea was not again coined, but was replaced by the sovereign, for, if the contents of the two coins were in the ratio of 21 to 20, the face values also were in the same ratio.

In like manner the silver standard which was introduced into Austria in 1858 by Freiherr Von Bruck, and lasted some months, was purely restoratory. The new silver gulden (" Austrian standard ") was, it is true, smaller than the old one, and as it happens, too, in the ratio of 20 to 21, but its face value was less in the same proportion, though the pieces had a different size.

Italy, which similarly harboured a paper standard for a long time, went back to a gold standard. The gold twenty-lire pieces were again valuta. This too is a restoratory change of standard if we assume that the State is absolutely prepared to make its payments in those gold pieces.

Most commonly in a restoration there is a return to the money which formerly had been valuta. No doubt this is a "resumption of specie payment," but that alone is not sufficiently definite. It is rather resumption of a specie payment of an old type.

Any kind of payment in hylogenic orthotypic money is specie payment. So in a restoratory change specie payments are in the same specie money which formerly had been valuta.

The restoration of a standard is, so to speak, the reflection as in a glass of a change in which an accessory kind of money with a negative agio is declared to be valuta. As the mirror exchanges the right and left sides, so the restoratory change of the standard calls back that kind of money which has been banished by the obstructional change.

In an obstructional change the State wishes to avoid the sacrifice necessary to maintain the earlier standard. Perhaps it will not, perhaps it cannot make the necessary sacrifice.

In a restoratory change, on the other hand, the State is ready to incur the great expense which, as a rule, such a measure demands. The State proceeds to restoration only if the financial position is favourable. For this reason a restoratory change always creates a most favourable impression of the financial position of the State, while an obstructional change exhibits the State as suffering financial distress, and the more so the greater the negative agio of the hitherto accessory money now to be made valuta. Hence there was only mild dismay, or even none at all, when France changed to a gold standard; the negative agio of the gold money was then very small. But every change to a paper standard causes great alarm, for, even if the paper was previously accessory, yet its negative agio was naturally the greatest possible. Public opinion only perceives large differences, and easily overlooks small ones. People only think that the standard has deteriorated when paper money becomes valuta in place of metal money and do not see that an obstructional change is also possible in a transition from one hylogenic standard to another hylogenic one (as in France under Napoleon III).

Of the exactory changes, which we have called novatory, and where there is no restoration, there are many recent examples. Very often the novatory change is to a gold standard, but the gold has nothing to do with it.

Germany's transition to a gold standard in 1871 and the following years is in point here. In earlier years we had a silver standard and there was no question of the piling up of gold pieces. Hence it was not an obstructional change, but the kind of exactory change which we call novatory; there was no restoration.

When Austria determined in 1892 to change from a

paper standard to a gold one, it was not a restoratory change, for that would have meant a return to the silver gulden of 1857. A new kind of money was made, namely, a gold piece valued in kronen, which was to be made valuta. That the half-gulden was now called a krone is of no importance. The kernel of the matter lies in the fact that a kind of money was made out of another hylic material than that of the ex-valuta silver gulden.

In this alone lay the novelty of the proceeding and its difference from a restoratory change.

Russia similarly changed from a paper to a gold standard and, moreover, without changing the name of the lytric unit. If they had gone back to the old silver rouble the change would have been restoratory, but, because there was a new gold rouble, it was a novatory change, just as in Austria.

Only exactory changes can be novatory in the strict sense of the word.

On the other hand, restoratory changes may also be obstructional, a circumstance which has only recently been observed with general astonishment.

When through the surprising fall of the London price of silver the internal (metallopolic) agio of the Austrian gulden sank in 1878 to zero, and even became negative, the coffers of the Austrian State filled up with silver gulden, that which since 1859 had been accessory. If now Austria had allowed this development to take a free course and after a time had declared that the silver gulden would again be treated as valuta, we should have witnessed a restoratory alteration of the standard by obstruction. On the contrary, in 1879 the free coinage of silver into silver gulden was discontinued.

A little earlier there was a similar situation in France, and, if there had been free coinage of silver into five-franc pieces, a similar obstructional restoration would have occurred, about the year 1876. This would have led back to the state of affairs before 1860. But there too the way was blocked by discontinuance of the coinage of silver.

A similar contingency was threatened in Russia, and was prevented in the like manner.

It is then entirely possible that an obstructional change may happen to lead to a restoration, no doubt under rare conditions, such as were caused by the quite unheard-of fall in the London price of silver.

Above we have also classified the changes according to a quite different point of view, namely of a rise, poise and fall.

There is always a fall when the alternation is obstructional, for this implies a piling up of accessory money, which again only occurs if the latter has a negative agio.

States do not always have a feeling against the falling movement; they bear with it when they permit an obstructional change (as, for example, in French bimetallism before 1876).

If the alteration does not mean a fall, it means a poise or a rise.   In Germany in 1871 there was a poise when the alteration was made from a silver to a gold standard ; this change was novatory because no gold standard had formerly existed.

Similarly Austria's change from a paper to a gold standard (1892) was in principle a poise.   Also it was novatory because no gold standard had formerly existed.

Both were cases of poise because the newly-made gold pieces introduced as accessory in the yet unaltered standard exhibited neither a negative nor a positive agio.   Notice that it depended on the then price of gold expressed in the yet unaltered standard of those countries, that is to say, in Germany on the then price of gold in silver money, in Austria on the then price of gold in paper money.

Such a poise, if it is also novatory, does not as a rule cause any disturbance, because people regard only the fact that at the moment it is introduced the new money (compared with its position before the change) is neither over-valued nor under-valued but of the same value.   Consequently from this point of view each falling change as well as each rising change is called disturbing.   Those who so judge are simply considering whether at the moment of the change the new money is appreciated or depreciated, and are satisfied if it is neither the one nor the other.

Finally, there is the case of a rise. The new valuta money (treated as accessory money on the existing standard) would exhibit a positive agio. If one returns to a money which formerly had been valuta, then the rising change is restoratory (as in England after 1815, in Austria in 1858, in Italy in 1903).

Such rising restoratory changes are very often judged to be " just," although they, as has been explained, are by no means " undisturbing." The standard to which return is made by the restoration is taken to be the one which is rightful, and so far the return appears to be legitimate. But why not a return to yet earlier forms? Is there a Statute of Limitations to be invoked against the standard which is to be restored? Usually it is a question of reintroducing a metal standard in the place of an intruded paper standard, and it may be that the judgment of "legitimacy" is made under the impression that paper standards are harmful, but metal standards useful. In any case (and it is the sole point here) this judgment is based on quite other grounds than the former one; they contradict one another.

Russia presented an instance of a rising change which was also novatory. When the paper rouble was converted into a gold rouble, equal to 2·16 marks at the Mint parity, this was not a poise, but a rise; it was also novatory, for, if restoratory, it would have led back to the silver rouble. Was this " undisturbing "? No, for the change was not a poise. Was it just? Not if only restoratory changes are just. From this we see how little is to be got from the popular judgments.

While hitherto we have only considered changes from one principal form of standard to another (we will call them ' radical changes '), there are still other changes of standard, which are carried out while the principal form is maintained and have only secondary effects. We will group them together as ' modifications.' To these belong the alterations in the hylogenic standard arising from the wearing down of the pieces and from changes in the hylogenic norm. As the hylogenic standards were the oldest, their modifications were the earliest to be observed and decried. Further, they have most frequently occurred with an argyrogenic standard, since the silver standard is older than the gold one. But the phenomena we refer to have nothing to do with silver as such.

At first we will assume that the hylogenic norm remains unchanged, so that we have to pay attention only to the wearing down of the pieces in circulation. If there are no hylodromic arrangements, the wearing down will manifest itself by a rise in the price of the hylic metal. A person who now judges the valuta money according to the hylic metal will say that the valuta money has fallen in value compared to the hylic metal, but then he has chosen a basis of his own for the concept of value. If he keeps to our basis he must say that the hylic metal rises in price in terms of the valuta money.

There would have been nothing to refute if it had been laid down that only the new pieces are valuta, and, as soon as the wearing down exceeds so much, the pieces will become accessory. Then everyone would have paid the State in worn pieces, while the State itself would always have paid in full-weight pieces. The so-called least current weight would not have decided whether the piece was valid or not, but only whether it was valuta or accessory. The deterioration of the currency could then have been prevented merely by the setting up of an apocentric least current weight. But in the more remote past the State was still in the " bonds of fiscality," and this was not done. The consequent alteration of the standard (so far as the price of the hylic metal now rose) was simply obstructional. The State paid out the worn pieces which were piling up in its chests; and so the eternal round began. Throughout the Middle Ages and during a considerable part of modern times this phenomenon has been observed in nearly all countries.

People thought it unavoidable, while it only occurs because the State resolves to pay out worn money again.

The alteration of the hylogenic norm, which is just as regularly observed, with hylogenic money, is of quite a different kind; it is always exactory and may be subdivided into novatory and restoratory changes.

In England, for instance, under almost every sovereign down to Elizabeth, the hylogenic norm for the penny (which at that time was valuta) was lowered.

At first the penny contained the $\frac{1}{240}$th part, and finally only the $697\frac{1}{2}$ part of a Tower pound of standard silver. The occurrence was exactory because it did not arise through a piling up, and novatory because it did not serve to re-establish a former system; lastly, the change was a fall because the lighter pieces, fitted into the old standard, would have shown a negative agio.

Through this the price of the hylic metal must rise, and this appears to be a debasement of the standard, because the natural man's feelings are autometallistic.

But conversely at times (say in England) a new coinage of pieces of the old Mint standard was carried out. This measure was also exactory, indeed remarkably so, because very burdensome to the exchequer; but it was restoratory, not novatory, and it was a rise, not a fall, for the new pieces fitted into the old monetary system would have shown a positive agio.

All this could have occurred just as well if gold had been the hylic metal of the valuta money.

Such altered relations to the hylic metal make a great impression on the metallists, for they think that payment properly consists in the quantity of metal delivered, while we hold as proved the Chartal, that is the proclamatory, validation of the pieces. But in the meantime it is clear to both parties that the price of the hylic metal will in any case be changed as much by the wearing down as by a lighter Mint standard; from this point of view the chief form of it is not affected though the standard changes, for the valuta money is always hylogenic and the hylic metal is the same as before.

We can now sum up what can be said about radical changes of the standard and modifications.

Are obstructional changes desired? Sometimes they are (as when France adopted a gold standard), sometimes they are not (as when in France in 1876 the silver standard threatened to return). On the other hand, exactory changes, being deliberately introduced, are desired by the State.

Are restoratory changes desired? Very often they are; but when the silver standard threatened to return in France and Austria, the restoration was forcibly prevented. On the other hand, novatory changes, because they are always exactory, are naturally always desired by the State.

Are falling changes desired? In France the change to a gold standard was a fall and was desired. On the other hand, falling changes, which exhibit clearly the financial embarrassment of the State, are always undesired.

The poise is commonly regarded by the public with

indifference (as in Germany's change to a gold
standard in 1871), yet it has a powerful influence on
the bullion market.

Finally, if the rise is not restoratory, but novatory,
as in Russia's change to a gold standard, why is it
taken in hand ? It cannot be perceived to be " just "
(as with the restoratory), nor is it " undisturbing "
(as the poise).

Let us now, keeping to the trade relations within
the country, inquire how such changes to a new
standard produce their effects there.

Undoubtedly they affect the bullion market, and in
many cases this effect can be demonstrated with
certainty.

Suppose that there is a change from an argyrodromic
standard to a chrysodromic one, then the price of
silver, which up till then has been fixed, will vary, and
the price of gold, which up till then has been fluctuating, will become fixed.

Everyone who is accustomed to buy or sell these
metals will be affected, mine-owners as sellers, the
industrial arts as buyers, then the buyers or sellers of
jewellery or utensils; in short, the whole " metallopolic " trade finds itself under new conditions.

Let us suppose the reverse, namely, the change from
a chrysodromic to an argyrodromic standard.   Then
the price of gold, which has till then been fixed, will
become fluctuating, and the price of silver will become
fixed.   All metallopolic business will be affected, but

in the opposite way, because the two metals have exchanged places.

Suppose there is a change from a metallodromic standard to an ametallodromic one; then immediately the prices of both metals will become fluctuating, while hitherto the price of only one of them had been.

But let us suppose the reverse, namely, the change from an ametallodromic standard to a metallodromic one; then the price of one metal will become fixed, that of the other remains variable as before.

All this always alters the conditions of metallopolic business, and will be keenly felt by those engaged in it, sometimes as a help, sometimes as a hindrance.

It must not be forgotten that the price of a metal always means its price in the money which is for the time being valuta. Before the change to the new standard the price therefore means the price in the then valuta money; after the change to the new standard, it means the price in the new valuta money.

The wave system of the sea becomes really more varied if a steamer is making its way, either rapidly or slowly, through the billows. But we may leave out the waves made by the steamer without appreciably altering the general view of the wave system.

So we can assert, in more general terms than before, the proposition that for internal trade, excluding the bullion business, the choice of the standard hardly matters at all, since it only produces secondary effects which vanish in the general welter of continuous price

P

changes. Daily there are a thousand kinds of disturbances, from new routes or canals, customs tariffs,
transport rates, the building of new ships, etc., which
now in this direction and now in that change the course
of trade little by little, and in the course of time
completely alter the picture. In the midst of all
this movement each person is seeking his own profit,
and in a thousand instances this or that price falls or
rises. But always the rise is due to the increased
power of the seller, the fall to his diminishing power;
and since prices are not expressed in terms of quantities
of metals, but of lytric units (marks, francs, roubles),
and since ultimately the payment is in valuta money,
it follows that the relation of this money to the metals
has no significance, for it is always quite clear which
kind of money is valuta. We express the prices in
lytric units,—not merely prices, but all liabilities
involving payment. The fact may be deplored but
cannot be denied, since nominalistic chartalism is now
once for all there in the world.

The change does no harm to internal trade, except
the bullion business, because of the amphitropic
position of the economic individual; he gives the
same kind of money as he receives. This is generally
true in all changes from one standard to another.
If the alteration is a fall, the apparent loss on receiving will be equalised by the corresponding gain on
paying. If the change is a rise, the apparent gain
on receiving will again be equalised by the correspond-

ing loss on paying. Then it comes to pass that alterations in the standard operate for internal trade, except the bullion business, only through secondary changes in an industrial community, in which thousands of conditions are constantly varying from other causes of far greater importance, so that those secondary changes of a few conditions do not play any particular part.

The usual views of the effects of the change to another standard on internal trade are quite in-adequate, so long as the amphitropic position of individuals is overlooked, and so long as our liabilities (in the chartalist sense) are left out of account. But, if both of these are taken into consideration, it is immediately clear that the effects of the change in standard are quite negligible, whether the change is down or up.

In the foregoing discussion the changes in the standard have only been described from the point of view of the disinterested observer; we have com-pletely avoided any explanation of the lytric policy which gives rise to such changes. Lytric policy deals with the machinery for means of payment; it includes everything which is determined in relation to it by Acts of Parliament, ordinances, or instructions, and is by no means limited (as the metallists think) to the mere production of the means of payment. There are, in addition, such administrative regulations for the system of payment as we have recognised in our functional classification of money. Lytric policy includes all of this, and the question is what aims govern this policy.

The metallists think all depends on the choice of a suitable standard. It appears to them suitable if the valuta money is specie; this requires a definite metal to be designated as hylic; they then demand hylodromy for this metal, and if all this is done they are satisfied, because they have the feeling that that metal is the measure of value. Everything, they think, will then be in order, assuming that no disturbance occurs in the ratio of the two metals.

The metallists are divided into three camps. The silver metallists want silver alone to be chosen as the hylic metal; they desire that silver specie money should be valuta, and that the price of silver within the country should be fixed by argyrodromy.

The gold metallists want gold alone to be chosen as the hylic metal; they desire that gold specie money should be valuta, and that the price of gold within the country should be fixed by chrysodromy.

Finally, the bimetallists want the hylic use of both gold and silver; they desire that there should be specie money of each of the two metals, that the specie money of that kind of metal which obtrudes itself obstructionally should be valuta, and that there should be hylodromy in relation to that metal.

All these metallistic views imply that before everything one should strive to give the creditor a " real " satisfaction on the occasion of every payment. The monometallists proceed quite logically; the one wishes above all to put silver into the hand of the creditor, the other wishes to give him gold. The bimetallists are not quite so logical. At the times of the change over from gold to silver or *vice versâ*, the nominality of the unit of money emerges; but the bimetallists pay no attention to this.

We see that all three have a horror of accessory money, which is generally of a paratypic (notal) kind.

In the matter of notes all metallists desire that they shall be convertible into valuta specie money; as regards notal coins, these must only be legal tender to a limited amount (*i. e.* made into small coin), or, if required, that they shall be convertible like notes. The motive is that, at any rate for the larger payments, " real " satisfaction shall be attainable.

If anywhere, by some political misfortune, autogenic paper money happens to come into the position of valuta, the metallist deplores the disappearance of " real " satisfaction and proposes as a remedy a restoratory change of standard; he can only conceive the autogenic paper money as a draft on the vanished valuta specie money. The metallist cannot grasp any other idea of this paper money, because he defines the unit of value as a quantity of metal.

The monometallist always holds the metal chosen by him to be the one which is subject to no fluctua-

tions in value. He is quite correct in that, for it
follows from the definition of unit of value which he
has chosen. The fluctuations in value of the other
metals are felt to be imperfections.

The bimetallist would consider it a great boon if
the ratio of the value of the two precious metals were
fixed, *e. g.* that a unit of weight of gold should be
worth 15½ units of weight of silver, or perhaps more.

All metallists indifferently, whichever of the three
camps they belong to, consider that the ratio of the
value of the precious metals is determined by the
quantities produced and sold. Greatly increased
silver production or an unusually great sale of silver
coins, which have lost their Chartal property, are, in
their opinion, the causes of the fall in the price of silver
since 1871. The earlier fixed rate is disturbed by
reasons arising from the bullion trade, and this, in the
opinion of the metallists, has the most serious consequences for the commercial relations between gold
countries and silver countries. It seemed more and
more clearly the fault of silver that the ratio was so
provokingly disturbed, and the gold metallist quietly
rejoices (and with some justice) that he has chosen a
more trustworthy metal.

"In the civilised world gold has triumphed; it is
the most suitable metal for hylic use, and specie gold
money alone is adapted for the position of valuta.
In this the true lytric policy is found, specie money
as valuta and gold as the hylic metal."

This conception of the metallists may be strongly recommended to public men. The man in the street easily understands that out of all the metals the best is chosen and then adhered to. Politicians will find nothing easier to defend than the gold standard. It is " sound," says common sense.

But it is an entirely different affair for the theorist to specify the real reason for the triumph of gold; he cannot find the effective ultimate reasons for the lytric policy of our States in the properties of metals; the real though certainly unconscious aim of lytric policy is rather to be found in international payments—payments between State and State.

CHAPTER III

§ 12. *The Inter-valuta Exchange*

THE relations of two neighbouring independent States are usually called international, though the problem concerns not nations but States. In every State it is valuta money which is the most important, and gives character to the monetary system. International relations in currency are therefore " inter-valuta relations," the relations of the valuta money of the one State to the valuta money of the other.

Inter-valuta relations are, roughly speaking, the " course of exchange." The new expression is better, as excluding the notion of a bill of exchange, here unimportant. By the value of bills of exchange we mean the price paid in the valuta money of the one country for this kind of effective claim on the valuta money of the other. By the inter-valuta value, on the other hand, we mean the price, expressed in the valuta money of the one country, paid for a given sum of the valuta money of the other country.

The expression course of exchange (*Wechselkurs*) is therefore too narrow for us. It implies that there are bills of exchange and that they are an object of trade. The market for this kind of trade is the Bourse, in countries with a highly developed economic system. The dealers are the so-called money-changers, or, in a higher stage of development, the bankers. Supply and demand affect the price of the exchange bills; it is therefore a trial of strength; the stronger of the two turns the scales. The value of bills does not originate with the authorities. There is no administrative power to regulate the settlement of bills of exchange. There is no State command to say, for instance, that a bill for 1000 francs is to be received for 810 marks in Germany. Laws and ordinances are only binding within the State that lays them down, on the assumption that our States are totally independent and have made no agreements as to currency.

Like that of the bills, the inter-valuta value is a purely mercantile phenomenon. It is the business of the money-changers, the bankers and the Bourse to settle by means of supply and demand how many lytric units of one standard are to be given for a lytric unit of the other. The price of the marks in francs—of the pound sterling in marks—of the rouble in marks, all this is fixed by the higgling of the market on the Bourse, like the price of wheat.

Here a very important contrast appears. Within a State the validity of the kinds of money is not a trade phenomenon, but rests on authority. A course of exchange, a price, only belongs to such kinds of accessory money as have become commodities, without thereby losing their validity.

In international trade, the validity reaches to the frontier but does not pass it. Foreign coins have no validity in our country, nor our coins abroad. The value of foreign coins expressed in the required valuta is decided by competition on the Bourse, not by authoritative act. The price so arrived at, whether of foreign money here or our money abroad, is then used as a point of departure for smaller transactions, and has therefore an appearance of authority, but this is only a commercial usage of subordinate interest. On the Bourse itself there is no authority controlling inter-valuta relations. According to this view it is easily seen how a franc is valued at 80, 81 or 82 pfennigs on the Bourse, or the rouble in Berlin at 2·14, 2·15 or 2·16 marks. These fluctuations are the necessary consequence of the independence of the States and their standards.

But we shall be told that there is a Mint par, and that Mint parity is in itself an inter-valuta parity. Tell me how many English sovereigns can be got out of a pound of fine gold, or in Germany how many twenty-mark pieces out of the same. I then calculate the Mint par, and this is the inter-valuta par for England and Germany. This widely held opinion is, as is easily seen, totally erroneous, and for two reasons. First, there is not always a Mint parity.

There is no Mint parity between England and Mexico, as silver is coined into valuta money in Mexico and gold in England. In the same way there is no Mint parity, if one country has a metal and the other a paper standard. If then there is sometimes a Mint parity and sometimes not, it could only sometimes, but not invariably, be the inter-valuta parity.

Secondly, even given a Mint par, as in the case of Germany and England, Mint parity does not imply inter-valuta parity. It does not follow from the undoubted Mint parity that the pound sterling has a fixed price in marks on the Berlin Bourse.

Mint parity, therefore, cannot be taken as equivalent to inter-valuta parity, because it may happen that the coins are not in each case valuta money.

A coin may be valuta money in one country and a coin of the same metal accessory in another. This was long the case of the English gold coins and the Italian twenty-lire pieces. The Mint par thus had no bearing on the English-Italian exchange, for in Italy the twenty-lire piece was accessory.

In the case of Mexico and England, it is clear that that silver country and this gold country could [1] have no Mint parity. Sometimes one is told that the exchange depends on the relative value of the precious metals. In this case a sort of independent existence is ascribed to this relation; it is supposed to be entirely settled by the barter of gold and silver.

[1] In 1905.

In that case it could be brought in to explain the exchange position of England and Mexico. But the supposed independence does not exist.

We therefore never speak of the relative value of the two metals in order to explain the inter-valutary exchange between silver and gold countries, or, as we shall see presently, we should be arguing in a circle.

In all cases it is safer to say that there is no par of exchange; *per se* it must be created by special arrangements which are not made when each State is only thinking of its internal circulation.

Anyone, therefore, who asks how many marks the franc, the rouble, the lira or the peseta is worth, can only be referred to the exchange bulletin. Mint parity is a different thing, and may occur now and then. Inter-valutary exchange parity, on the other hand, is created anew each day.

Childish inexperience may object that there can then be no international trade. If there is no fixed relation between mark and rouble, how can business be transacted between these two countries? As a matter of fact, business is made more difficult, but is not stopped. It is impossible to make an accurate calculation as to profits, but this does not prevent all business. The merchant is daring, and knows how to set off some risks against others.

My own view is that the first given condition of things is a fluctuating inter-valutary exchange. Theory does not need to explain why it is sometimes fluctuating, but rather why it is ever fixed. Those who start from the theory that the exchange is normally fixed can never understand its variations. It is easy to understand its occasional stability, if one starts from the opposite assumption.

The inter-valutary exchange in all cases depends on the sum total of the transactions between two countries which entail payment in either direction. It is the expression of the momentary gap between supply and demand in respect of the foreign currency on the Bourse. The question how many marks the pound sterling is worth in Berlin depends on the balancing of supply and demand. Supply and demand arise from unsettled business obligations and speculation. The inter-valutary exchange is determined by business settlements, which give rise to payments on one side or the other, and also by forecasts of future business conditions. The exchange is therefore a psychological phenomenon; it depends on acts of will in the past which have given rise to these unsettled transactions, and also on opinions as to future business relations. It cannot be ascertained by any technical consideration of the material of the valuta pieces, because its origin is not Chartal and technical, but mercantile and psychological.

It might be feared that the exchange between two countries would make wild jumps, all the more as we see that the incalculable factor of moods and feelings is involved. It is historically true that large

fluctuations have occurred, especially when disturbances in business relations and in moods and feelings
have given the occasion. Such critical times belong
to actual experience, and should not be pushed into
the corner as exceptions. For the theorist there
are no exceptions. On the other hand, owing to the
varied complexity of business relations, large alterations of their general tendency are very rare, and a
direct reversal of opinion only takes place under
extraordinary circumstances. The exchange has, as
a rule, a certain inertia, which is only shaken by
great events. Its psychological origin allows great
fluctuations without necessarily entailing them.

In order to give to the psychological view a name
which suggests to the mind the sum-total of mercantile relations, we say that the inter-valutary exchange
between two countries is explained *pantopolically*.
This word indicates that we are referring to the fixing
of a price for the valuta money of one country on the
Bourse of the other, settled by the total liabilities
and by the moods and feelings on which the settlement of price is based. All this is compressed in the
proposition : The inter-valutary exchange is a
pantopolic phenomenon.

The influence of the bullion dealers is admitted,
but it is denied that the question is for them alone.
It is most plainly pointed out that the exchange
cannot be clearly grasped through the metallistic
conception of money.

Pantopolic relations which fix the rate of exchange can only be understood in detail by one who keeps perpetually in view the balance of payments between the two countries. This needs an uncommonly rich experience of Bourse transactions, such as falls to the lot of few, and which naturally can only relate to given countries and times.

Now and again the view seems to have dawned upon men that money has " a certain value " even if it does not consist of metal and is not hylodromically regulated. More exactly, the valuta money of a country must not be absolutely hylogenic, and in the country there must not be absolute hylodromy; then (under these conditions) the money lacks a fixed relation to a hylic metal. In spite, however, of the fact that no metal can be found in relation to which the valuta money has a fixed value, it is not valueless. It has " a certain value " as a Chartal means of payment.

This reasoning implies, in the first place, the idea that properly speaking the hylic metal is the commodity for comparison when we would find the value of money. To this autometallistic notion the Chartal theory gives the lie, affirming on the contrary that monetary systems are possible where the hylic metal has no fixed price.

The Chartal theory holds that money—even when made of paper and in the absence of hylodromy—is not ' a thing of nothing '; it is still the instrument for transferring the units of value from one hand to the other, and answers perfectly for internal circulation.

Should it be asked if such money has " a certain value," we must first agree as to the object of comparison. If a metal is chosen, the answer has been already given—the money has not a fixed value in terms of metal, but as each metal continues to have a price of a kind, though a fluctuating price, so also that money has a value, though a fluctuating one, in terms of the metal with which it is compared.

Presumably, however, it is not metal that is thought of, but the valuta money of another country, especially a foreign hylodromically regulated money. It can therefore be said that papyroplatic money without hylodromic regulation has yet " a certain value " in terms of the hylodromically regulated money of another country. Therefore it is not hylodromy alone which gives the money of a country " a certain value " in terms of the money of another country.

Very true, but the champion of the Chartal theory takes all this for granted, for to him the hylodromic control of money does not seem a necessary basis, but only a concomitant circumstance. Moreover, he can say how that certain value is fixed. It depends on the pantopolic relations of the two countries, for that " certain value " is simply the inter-valutary exchange.

According to the pantopolic theory there can be no inter-valutary par, and no fixed relation between mark and franc, mark and rouble, mark and pound sterling, for these are lytric units and not coins.

Yet everyone talks of the par of inter-valutary exchange and of the occasional departures from it, " above par " and " below par." The explanation is simple. We have only laid it down that countries with independent monetary systems do not *per se*, that is, as a consequence of these systems, have a par of exchange. There is, however, a State lytric policy which, added to the State monetary systems, demands and realises a parity. Such a policy is common enough. Very often it is pursued unconsciously, and very often its aims are attained, as it were, automatically. On the other hand, the parity is always the result of *lytropolitic* intention. The franc is not *per se* worth 81 pfennigs of German money, but there is a policy at work to keep it at this value. So with the rouble, which was not in 1903 really worth 2·16 marks, but there was a policy to keep it so.

The policy can be successful for long periods together, keeping the exchange steady with small fluctuations up or down. Sometimes crises occur which prove that the parity was only a political aim, suddenly made unattainable.

The position here laid down is the corner-stone of the theory of inter-valutary exchange. As the concept of chartality is the key to the understanding of the monetary system of the individual State,

Q

the *pantopolic* view of the inter-valutary exchange
is the key to the understanding of international
currency relations.

It follows that if inter-valutary exchange parity
is aimed at, it needs an exchange control of the
administration to keep it up.

It is as with the fixed price of metal within the
country. Hylodromy needs the continuous action
of a hylodromic administration. The action which
fixes the inter-valutary parity may be called *exodromic*.
A lasting inter-valutary parity is the result of
exodromic control.

There is a suggestion in it of hylodromic control.
The two are alike in laying down rules for trade,
but without any view to profit.

As soon as a given parity is set up, the exchange
value of the moment can be judged as above or below
par. The question is now how a given parity is
selected, either for judging the present exchange
value or for actual realisation of the par itself.

It may be the Mint par, when there is one; it
may be that the exchange rate of a given time in
history is treated as par. Often, however, the choice
is guided merely by convenience and this or that
exchange value is arbitrarily set up as par.

In all three cases the choice depends on a decision
of the State; and this decision is particularly instructive when it rests on a Mint parity. It is so easily
brought about and so easily understood that parity

is thought of by many only in connection with Mint
parity. But that is not the only possible choice.
The parity aimed at is a conception formed by
inter-valutary exchange policy; it does not flow
from the very nature of the currency systems of the
two countries in themselves.

When Austria on the one hand and Russia on the
other had a purely paper currency, there was no par,
unless by a decision of the State.

So was it when Germany had a silver standard
and England a gold one. As soon as Germany as
well as England had a gold standard, there was only
a par because of a decision of the State to regard
the exchange which corresponded to Mint par as
parity and to maintain it by special arrangements.
A different par was, however, conceivable. Once
a given state of exchange has been declared to
be par, the actual exchange of the foreign valuta
money may be either above or below par. The
foreign money has then Agio or Disagio (discount);
or, differently expressed, positive or negative agio.

This valuta agio is a phenomenon of international
business, and has nothing to do with the domestic
agio we have previously discussed. In trade
between two States the valuta money of the one
can have an agio in relation to the par. This foreign
agio, whether positive or negative, is no result of
conditions in the bullion market in particular, but
is always pantopolic in origin. It is a pity that in

commercial circles the word agio is used for both
phenomena. In the foreign agio, it is a question
of two given States and their valuta, not of accessory
money.

In Austria in 1878 the domestic agio on the silver
gulden disappeared. No one took any notice, because
the gulden was an accessory coin. Foreign trade
remained undisturbed. But when, soon after 1892,
the foreign agio disappeared, the Austrians felt
themselves, as far as foreign trade was concerned,
at the goal of their ambition.

In all discussions on these deeply important
matters no one has laid down the distinction in
principle between the two kinds of agio, because
all were still hampered by the metallistic view of
currency.

Once again we declare our principle : The domestic
agio depends on the bullion trade and is essentially
metallopolic. The foreign agio can only arise when
parity has been set up as the goal or norm, and then,
like the inter-valutary exchange itself, it is essentially
pantopolic.

The domestic agio, if on accessory silver coins
and positive, can be called silver agio, or, if on accessory
gold, gold agio ; for it arises from the price of those
metals.

The foreign agio, on the other hand, can only
occasionally be called gold or silver agio, and then
in quite another sense. It is always the agio on

foreign valuta money. If this foreign money chances to be of the gold standard, the agio is a gold agio; if of the silver standard, a silver agio. If the foreign money is neither, the agio cannot be called either a gold or silver agio.

If English valuta money has an agio from the point of view of Germany, the right phrase is that English money has an agio. In speaking of foreign agio we need to name the country, not the metal.

For the domestic agio we must name the metal. In this case it is immaterial whether this metal is kept at a fixed price in a foreign country or not. We regard the exchange as a pantopolic phenomenon, *i. e.* we see in it the price of a foreign valuta money in terms of our own valuta money. Price and value are in our eyes always " lytro-basic," *i. e.* they are related to a means of payment, in doubtful cases to a valuta means of payment. We never think of a metal as an object of comparison.

This view, to which we are absolutely driven in order to explain the facts, has a remarkable consequence. The value of a foreign money—the English, for example—expressed in German money is a result of general trade relations. There is no previously existing *a priori* relation of the pound sterling to the mark. The exchange value of the pound sterling at a given moment, expressed in our lytric unit, the mark, is always created by trade, more accurately by business relations. There is not a course of exchange which

precedes trading; the exchange arises as the result
of the trading. This is the meaning of the pantopolic
point of view. The correctness of the theory is
proved by the fact that it explains everything. The
contrary view of the metallists—that there is an
exchange par on which trade is based as an antecedent
is quite wrong. Trade only presupposes that there
is a course of exchange, not that there is a fixed one,
and traders use the exchange, whatever it may be, as
the starting-point of their calculations. They start
from to-day's exchange and help to make to-morrow's.

The pantopolic explanation of the exchange is
quite unacceptable to the metallist, but it follows from
the Chartal system, from the fact that we no longer
have pensatory means of payment; and it alone
explains the exchange in all instances. As " measure
of value," metals are finally deposed—not by theory,
but by the fact that autometallism no longer exists.
" Autometallism would be so much simpler, easier
to grasp and handle," you say. Yes, but it has
ceased to exist, and it was not the theorist who
killed it; it was the course of history. The theorist
has only to show what has happened and how we must
adapt ourselves to the new situation. This new
situation needs an *exodromic* control to secure fixed
exchanges as between different countries.

§ 13. *Ratio of Gold and Silver*

London has long been the leading silver market in the civilised world. The price of silver is quoted there on the basis of the standard ounce, the number of pence paid each day per ounce being published. It is thus clear how many silver units of weight are given for each gold unit of weight, and indeed for the gold in the English sovereign, which is kept at a fixed price in the general gold market by metallo-dromic control.

What fixes the London price of silver? Is it an isolated phenomenon or does it reflect other economic processes? Is it under human control or is it forced on us by fate?

The case is simplified if we take two exactly opposite extreme instances, imagining circumstances, like a school text-book.

Suppose that all civilised countries had introduced a gold standard like the English. We will assume that for some time the stock of accessory silver money remains unaltered. Those States neither try new silver in order to coin it, nor discard old silver money to sell it as a commodity. The currency of those countries is therefore entirely without influence on the London silver market, giving rise neither to demand nor supply.

In this first extreme instance the London silver price is made just like the price of tin or lead or any other metal, gold excepted, indeed like the price of all other commodities which have no connection with the currency. The only questions now are (a) how much silver is offered for sale, either fresh from the mines or by the disposal of silver articles; and (b) how much silver must be bought in industry for art, photography, etc. The silver price is fixed by demand and supply without any lytropolitic influence, i. e. without any influence on matters connected with the currency system.

Take the opposite hypothesis, that silver is no longer employed in industry. Silver is still mined, but is only used for currency and only in one country, let us say, India. India has a dromic silver standard (as before 1893). All silver will then be used only for free coinage into Indian rupees. Silver would then have a price on the London market determined entirely by the Anglo-Indian Exchange. The ounce of silver could be turned into so many rupees;—we have excluded all other uses. Its price depends on the rupee exchange, which is settled pantopolically, i. e. by all the circumstances which involve payments between England and India in either direction.

In the first of the two cases the London silver price would depend only on industry. Influence from inter-valutary exchange of any country would be excluded, as we have assumed that there were no countries whose currency system could influence the silver markets.

In the second case, the London silver price would depend entirely on the Indian Exchange, for we have assumed that silver is not used in industry, and secondly that India has, and alone has, a silver standard. In actual fact neither extreme case occurs. Besides the gold standard countries, England and Germany, there are silver standard countries (Mexico before 1919 and India before 1893). It is, moreover, inconceivable that silver should ever entirely cease to be used in industry. The London silver price depends neither entirely on industry nor entirely on the inter-valutary exchange, but on a complex combination of the two.

We have established one important principle. It is not possible to regard the price of silver as purely industrial, so that industrial grounds could be alleged with a good conscience as the explanation of the English valuta exchange position with regard to countries of the silver standard. It is wrong to say the rupee exchange is high or low because the London price of silver is high or low. The Anglo-Indian valuta exchange itself influences this price, and we should be moving in a circle.

It would, however, be no less incorrect to explain the London price of silver only by the English valuta exchange with the silver countries, for it is clear that industrial conditions also operate. Industrial causes, however, are much weaker in determining the silver price than those which spring from the valuta exchange. The height of the sea on the coast is affected mainly by the tides, but also to a small extent by the wind.

Suppose that England with its gold standard and India with its silver standard were the only two countries concerned. The silver price is fixed at 60 pence in London. Now sellers appear in the market who are satisfied with 59 pence an ounce for a given quantity of bullion. The buyers of this cheap silver convert it into rupees and offer it as a means of payment for India. The rupee exchange then falls a little, but as it is settled pantopolically it does not depend only on the fact that these people have bought their silver cheap, but on a thousand other and earlier circumstances, which still have an effect. The exchange may fall a little, but not necessarily from 60 to 59.

The case is analogous when the sellers of silver can from industrial reasons get 61 pence an ounce, because there are buyers who are willing to pay that price. This high rate will cause a certain number of rupees to be melted. The rupee exchange would perhaps rise a little, but not to 61 pence, for there are plenty of other causes at work.

Those who imagine that the rupee exchange follows the silver price (whether 59 or 61) are conceiving the valuta exchange as depending only on the bullion market, an error impossible to those who hold the pantopolic view of the valuta exchange.

In face of the thousand other transactions alongside of the silver transactions, the rupee exchange is little affected by the latter.

The question turns on the comparative importance of the business provoked by special opportunities in the bullion trade and the much greater volume of business entirely independent of it. It is almost always right to dismiss the former as unimportant and to say that industrial disturbances of the price of silver do occur, but they are not strong enough to affect the Indian Exchange and soon disappear after raising a few ripples; the London silver price is in the main determined by the Indian valuta exchange.

We arrive best at this conclusion if we remember that there were other countries besides India with a silver standard, as, for instance, Germany before 1871. In that case if, owing to increased production of silver or a greater use of silver in industry, the price of silver temporarily rose or fell, transactions in silver would be provoked, of the sort described. But, while they previously influenced the pantopolic relations with India, they now influence those with India and with Germany. If they had little weight before, they have still less now and the ripples they cause are scarcely noticeable.

We have here started from the assumption that silver in England sank to 59 pence or rose to 61 pence, with the result that the Anglo-Indian valuta exchange soon absorbed the fluctuation without being much disturbed.

The London silver price is, however, much more closely connected with the valuta exchange between England and the silver countries, for the simple assumption of a rise to 61 pence or a fall to 59 pence from industrial causes is not permissible. The case is rather to be summarised as follows :

As long as, in addition to England with its gold standard, there are countries which absorb silver into their currency at a fixed price without limit—*e.g.* India before 1893 or Germany before 1871—silver can always be disposed of at a fixed price in the standard of the silver countries. Every pound of silver, for example, can be transformed into thirty thalers. This circumstance is the most important factor in settling the London price, for the countries with free coinage of silver are buyers who never refuse and whose prices never vary.

Any quantity of silver coming on the London market can be sold to the silver countries, at a fixed price in their standard, *e.g.* one pound for thirty thalers. It is therefore impossible for the London silver price to fall below thirty thalers for the pound fine.   On the other hand, it cannot go much above thirty thalers as long as it is possible to get thaler pieces from Germany, as a pound fine is contained in thirty such pieces.

But the question is now what silver costs in London,

not in thalers but in pence. This is determined quite simply according to the German-English valuta exchange, *i. e.* pantopolically. The silver price in London accordingly has almost always been the reflection of the valuta exchange between England and the silver countries, so long as there are such countries at hand; and this is owing to the fact that silver in those countries has a lytric position and is not a mere commodity like lead or tin.

Assume that silver production is largely increasing; the silver price does not fall in the way the price of other metals would fall under similar circumstances; but the silver price is depressed in a roundabout way by the corresponding influence of the English valuta exchange on the silver countries.

The case would be analogous if there were a large increase in the industrial consumption of silver. Then the price would not rise, in the same way as it would for other metals, but in a roundabout way through the effect of the corresponding alteration of the English valuta exchange on the silver countries.

Alterations in silver production or consumption do affect the London price of silver, but not in the same way as with the lytrically-indifferent metals, but always in the roundabout way of the valuta exchanges. The London price is determined pantopolically; and industrial conditions, such as increased production or consumption of silver, are only effective in so far as they co-operate in the whole complex pantopolic movement.

The case of gold is entirely similar. As gold in certain countries has free coinage at fixed prices, when there is increased production the metal is stocked; in the opposite case of increased consumption, it is taken out of the stock.

The ratio of silver to gold is therefore not immediately settled by the industrial production or consumption of each of the two metals, as would be the case with lead or tin. The ratio of the two precious metals is first recognised by its effect on the valuta exchange between gold countries and silver countries. The valuta exchange, however, does not depend entirely on those effects, but on innumerable other circumstances. Alterations in the bullion stocks of civilised countries do not, therefore, immediately determine the ratio of silver and gold. It is not true that increased gold production straightway depresses gold in terms of silver without any intermediate stage. The question is whether increased gold production makes the money of the gold countries fall in terms of the money of the silver countries, which happens sometimes, or whether increased silver production depresses the currency of the silver countries, which also happens on occasion.

But above all remember that political feelings may raise or depress the money of the gold countries in relation to that of the silver countries, and then the ratio of the precious metals will be affected without any change having occurred in the industrial use of these metals.

About 1850 and onwards there was a great increase in gold production in California. What is easier than to suppose that the ratio of gold and silver should therefore move against gold, as was in fact the case? People argue that there is more gold, while the supply of silver is unaltered; gold, therefore, naturally becomes cheaper from the standpoint of the silver countries.

But notoriously the later increase of gold production in Australia and Africa, which was on a far larger scale, did not make gold cheaper, from the standpoint of the silver countries. The reason, people might say, was that silver production had risen or silver consumption fallen to correspond. This must be the judgment of those who wish to explain the ratio of silver and gold only through production and consumption. That is the purely industrial view, to which we oppose the inter-valutary view with the question, " Could the Californian gold depress sterling in terms of the German thaler or the Indian rupee ? "

Let us suppose all the new Californian gold was brought to England and converted into money at the rate of £3 17s. 9d. an ounce. It was handed in at the Bank, which paid the fixed price in banknotes. Happy is the man who has the quantity theory for his guide; he says that English money was disproportionately increased, and therefore lost ground in the exchange as compared with the money of the silver countries. But we do not admit this deduction from the mere quantity of money. There must be some definite trade transactions which depress the pound in terms of the money of the silver countries. Something like the following may have happened. Those who have handed the newly produced gold for English money must invest that money. Perhaps the rate of interest in England is too low for them. Germany, before 1871, had a higher rate which could be enjoyed by purchase of German State securities. Demand, therefore, arose for this article of German export, and this tended to raise the German silver coinage a little, just as any other fresh article of export would do. English gold money then sinks a little in terms of German silver. We do not assert that it was so, but only that these dealings were possible and that the effect indicated could only be produced by new transactions of this sort, or else the valuta exchange could not alter; but the altered valuta exchange at once alters the ratio of the two precious metals. This is our " business theory."

It is easy to see that the alterations of the valuta exchange arising in this way are proportionately less the more silver countries there are alongside of the gold country, England. For the effect of these newly-developed transactions must be distributed among all the silver countries, forming as they do one connected whole. It is as if a given force is brought to bear on larger masses, and therefore causes less disturbance than before.

The chief reason why before 1871 the so-called ratio of the precious metals fluctuated so little was the large extent of the countries which then had the silver standard.

About the end of the fifties of the last century, when the price of silver rose in proportion to gold, London had silver prices of 62 pence, while 60½ pence had been the usual price before. Now I allow that the increased gold production of California had contributed to this; but I add that the effect must be produced through trade dealings correspondingly depressing the English valuta exchange with the silver countries. It must, however, be remembered that the businesses independent of gold production, in so far as they altered the exchange themselves, played a part in altering the ratio of the precious metals. The following instances may be given.[1]

The Indian Mutiny of 1857 forced the English to carry on a long war in India. The enormous expenditure involved caused a large demand for rupees, which had to be bought with English money regardless of cost. This drove up the exchange of the rupee; and the silver, which was convertible at a fixed rate

[1] From Ellstaetter and O. Heyn.

R

into rupees, followed the movement. It was not because the price of silver rose that the exchange of the rupee increased, but because, when the rupee became dearer, silver rose with it.

There were therefore two totally independent sets of circumstances at work. Californian gold production set on foot trade transactions which depressed the English exchange in the silver countries; the Indian Mutiny created business which raised the value of the Indian silver money in terms of English gold. Both circumstances worked in the same direction—gold went back in value compared with silver. The inhabitants of silver countries talked of the fall of gold, those of gold countries of the rise of silver. The amount of the difference, however, was small when compared with that of more recent times. The price of silver rose from 60½ pence only to 62 pence, because of the wide prevalence of the silver standard. So long as there are countries with a silver standard as well as countries, like England, with a gold standard, the ratio of the precious metals is chiefly a reflection of the valuta exchange between gold countries and silver countries. This exchange is settled pantopolically. Alterations in production and industrial use of the precious metals affect the valuta exchange in a roundabout way by giving rise to certain new businesses, which are added to the number producing the total pantopolic effect. But besides these, the businesses independent of bullion production and industrial use also leave their mark on the so-called ratio of the precious metals.

At the same time, we maintain that the ratio of the precious metals is an *exodromic* phenomenon, as long as there are silver countries as well as gold countries. Exodromic means "concerned with the movement of the exchange between the home country and the foreign." Production and consumption of those metals only have effect in so far as they create business which is exodromically felt.

After 1871, and more especially since 1876, the London silver price sank from 60½ pence almost without pause to quotations as low as 23 pence. Can the fall of the London silver price be explained exodromically?

Let us keep in mind that Germany, Scandinavia, Holland and also (in 1876) France had altered their currency to a gold standard. This meant an extraordinary diminution of countries with a silver standard, especially as the question is not one of area but of the extent of their trade relations with the gold countries. Everyone believes that the amount of silver produced by the mines at this time had increased. This may be allowed to have a tendency to depress the silver price, with the proviso that this tendency must express itself . exodromically. But, if we leave out this increase in production, the view now to be presented becomes all the more striking.

The fact that important countries like France,

Germany and Scandinavia went on to the gold standard made superfluous many silver current coins there, which up to that time had been valuta. Superfluous though they were, France had not sold her five-franc pieces as bullion, and Germany had retained her thalers. Let us assume, for shortness, that all these States had kept their coins, only with a different function, that is, had made them accessory money. In that case this transition to the gold standard would have thrown no silver on the market.

We again simplify the proceedings, but always against our own case. We wish to show why the London silver price sank to such depths, and deny ourselves the support of the fact of increased production and the sale of disused coin, though both of these obviously contributed.

It seems to me possible to see why there was a heavy fall in the London price of silver, quite apart from these contributory causes.

Anyone bringing silver to the London market, say in the year 1890, is able to convert it into Indian rupees and also into Mexican pesos. (We will leave the Far East out of account.) He will therefore get at least as many pence per ounce as correspond to the rupee or peso price in pence. This fixes the lower limit. At one time there had been a thaler exchange (before 1871), the franc exchange before 1860, in short the exchange of all the countries of the silver standard. Now the Anglo-Indian and the

Anglo-Mexican exchange formed the only lower limit for the seller of silver.

The rupee exchange and the peso exchange since 1876 would have sunk, even without increased silver production or the sale of disused pieces. That is my thesis.

The Indian rupee and the Mexican peso from 1871, and especially since 1876, sank owing to pantopolic reasons. This is proved by the events of 1893. The Indian Mints then ceased to accept silver for free coinage. At the time of the closing of the Mints the rupee exchange was about 15 pence. It did not rise in consequence of this act, but remained at 15 pence and even sank to 12–13 pence. We must come to terms with this fact, surprising to writers who start from the idea that the fall was due to the cheaper silver forcing itself in. We do not share their astonishment, for we hold that the rupee fell from pantopolic reasons. If such reasons still continued —which we have to prove—why should the closing of the Indian Mints raise the rate of the rupee exchange? It is unquestionable that it did not rise; and just for that reason we conclude that the fall of the rupee was not due to silver becoming cheap and dragging down the rupee, but the London price of silver fell from 1871 to 1893 and afterwards, because the rupee exchange weakened on pantopolic grounds. The London silver price followed the movement because the rupee exchange had always set its lower limit. Because this limit of value sank, the silver price also declined.

Here, however, we must give a brief sketch of the pantopolic relations between England and India. In the earlier period, from the time of the Indian Mutiny, England was forced to make enormous purchases of Indian currency. Millions of rupees had to be bought at any price, and the rupee then rose to two shillings (24 pence). In the second period the compulsion no longer existed. Since 1893 precisely the opposite state of affairs prevailed. The Indian Government was forced each year to buy large amounts of English currency and pay for them in rupees. The English money was needed for the interest on the Indian State debt, which is for the most part expressed in sterling, for the interest on the railway debt, also in sterling, and for the pensions of English officers and officials, also paid in English money. The English money for these must be found at any cost. The Indian Government sells rupee bills by tender each Wednesday, getting sometimes 15, 14, 12 pence for the rupee, perhaps, on occasion, 16 pence; but it has never contrived to get 20 pence, still less 24 pence for the rupee. This state of affairs explains the rupee exchange, which is so far lower than in the halcyon days when it was 24 pence. The Indian Government wishes the halcyon days back again because it no longer buys rupees but sells them.

Of course, this is only one among the many facts that determine the Indian exchange, but it is all-important, as the others are not strong enough to counteract it. India holds very little of the English National Debt, which would give it a claim on interest payments. It does not export sufficiently to England to balance the English imports. Quite apart from the question of Government action, India has to offer rupees to pay for English goods. As there is no fixed parity between the rupee and sterling, the valuta exchange depends on the balance of payments, and that is against India.[1] This explains the low quotation for the rupee in pence and the low price of silver in London. All this when there is no question of increased silver production nor of sale of disused coins in the London market. This survey seems to prove, so far as full proof is possible within the limits of a summary, that pantopolic conditions alone would sufficiently account for the fall of the rupee exchange. But there are yet other determining factors.

In the first period, when the rupee exchange was rising, the rise was very small compared with the fall in the second period. Now hear the reason for this extremely striking difference. In the first period, roughly 1857 to 1871, there were many silver countries besides India—Germany, for a time also France, Scandinavia, and the Netherlands. At this time a

[1] 1905.

rise of the rupee exchange meant an increased demand for the money of the other silver countries, as it was easily convertible into rupees. If the English Government offered 24 pence for the rupee, instead of 22 pence or 23 pence, it could cover its demands with French, German or Scandinavian money, without needing to offer 25 pence or over for the rupee.

In the second period the case was different. The countries we named had left the silver standard for the gold standard. India, continuing to buy English money with rupees, lost the support it formerly had in these countries, with only perhaps Mexico left to it. It could not get German, French or Dutch money (with an exchange little affected), wherewith to purchase English money. These means of lightening the fall of the rupee had disappeared. It was this lessened number of silver countries which caused the fall of the rupee to have a much stronger effect than before, and was the reason of the fall of the London price of silver in the second period from 60½ pence to 23 pence, while in the first period the rise was only from 60½ pence to 62 pence.

In Mexico in the second period the conditions were similar to those of India. It had State loans in the currency of the gold countries and railway loans in sterling, large imports from gold standard countries and comparatively small production of goods which could be exported to Europe. Mexico, therefore, could not support India, but its own peso exchange fell from pantopolic reasons in just the same way as the rupee exchange.

Not till India and Mexico should be able to prescribe the conditions under which the inhabitants of the gold standard countries should buy their goods could the exchange of the rupee and the peso rise again—that is, rise of itself without Government interference.

The ratio of gold and silver was also affected by French bimetallism, or rather by French lytric policy, in virtue of which France sided sometimes with the silver countries, sometimes with the gold. It is usually thought that under the French Constitution of 1803 such a transition could take place automatically. True, it was carried out unintentionally and inadvertently, because it was then supposed that the State should only attend to its own financial interests and not to those of commerce. On closer inspection it would seem that for the State to move from the silver group to the gold group, or the other way round, it must make a deliberate decision. For the whole thing turns on whether its silver money or its gold money should be treated as valuta; and this needs an administrative order to the State pay-offices, including the Bank of France. It is conceivable that the State should in its decision follow the line of its financial advantage, but this is not necessary; it might let reasons of trade policy prevail and bear the financial loss thus entailed.

Up to 1860 France treated its silver as valuta; final apocentric payments were made in definitive silver current money. So long as this continued, France belonged to the then very large group of silver countries. But because England, as we have seen, continually offered higher prices for silver, including French valuta money (up to 62 pence for the standard ounce), France began to treat its definitive gold current money as valuta. Immediately the silver coins, now become accessory, acquired an agio in France—they became a commodity for export to England. Thus a rich source of silver supply was opened for England, preventing the further rise of silver prices, and having a depressing effect on the London silver market.

This is the epoch when French currency policy really helped to stabilise the price of silver. Though people do not see it, this happened also at other times, for it needs a deliberate decision to treat gold money as valuta—a decision which was adopted at first merely because it was financially profitable for France.

Later, after the year 1871, or rather after the disturbances of the war were over, and Germany had gone over to the gold standard, the position altered. Silver in London became cheaper than before—from pantopolic reasons, and France would have been able to make its silver money again valuta. This would have been financially quite profitable;

but France, on grounds of trade policy, did not wish to rejoin the silver group. In 1876 accordingly the free coinage of silver came to an end. The swing of the pendulum, till then taken as a matter of course, no longer took place; bimetallism fell into abeyance, and France ceased to depress the silver market.

The celebrated " stabilising influence " of French bimetallism was therefore only once called into action. When the second opportunity was offered, France voluntarily renounced the use of this device.

And now we seem to have extracted the tiny grain of truth actually contained in the theory of bimetallism.

Soon India and Mexico too will go over to the gold standard, on the basis of the valuta exchange parity prevailing at the time, that is according to the measure of their commercial strength. They will then have to take deliberate and conscious measures to maintain the parity chosen, and they may perhaps succeed.

If at some later time silver loses its position as valuta in the Far East and there are no longer any countries with a silver standard, then and only then will the London silver price be fixed exactly in the same way as that of lead and tin; the price of silver will be something totally independent of currency systems. But even so it will always be wrong from the historical point of view to explain the earlier fluctuations of the valuta exchange between gold and silver countries on the basis of the then prevailing silver price, conceived as fixed by purely industrial reasons. This is a heresy which perhaps will be scarcely conceivable in future times.

§ 14a. Exodromic Administration

Our money abroad has not validity by law, but has a value as a commodity. This proposition holds good for our money of every kind, including valuta money, which, as we have seen, is precluded by the notion of valuta from being used as a commodity at home.

What value then has our valuta money (the only one important for our purpose) abroad? So long as we consider foreign countries as totally independent in their currency, our valuta money can have two kinds of value in accordance with the use chosen by the holder.

The holder can use the piece of money platically. Then only the material and weight of the coin are considered. If the piece is of paper, there can, of course, be no question of this; if, however, it is made of aluminium it can be used as a piece of this metal, and the same if it is of silver or gold. Or the holder can offer the piece to the money-changer, who will then consider the fact that with this piece of money payments can be made to Germany. The piece of money abroad has therefore a value corresponding to the supposed inter-valutary exchange parity, and the money-changer will make his offer accordingly. The exchange parity is not fixed, but the money-changer will fix a price which secures him against loss.

These two estimates of the value do not go together. They cannot be added to each other because they are mutually exclusive. The owner can choose either use, and he chooses the more profitable. Our valuta money abroad, therefore, has the value which is given by the higher of the two estimates, the platical or the lytrical. Here the lytric judgment is also a commercial one, for the money-changer " speculates "; he does not know in the least what the Bourse price will be in the future when he sends back the piece of money to the country of its origin. This price on the Bourse in the future is settled by the conditions in the future, including the profitable use of this piece. The money-changer would be a very bad man of business if he did not feel this by a sort of instinct; it does not matter whether or not he could formulate the instinct in words. He asks, therefore, a small fee not only for changing the money, but also as cover for the risk he runs. There is no parity in the nature of things for the inter-valutary exchange of two countries, so long as we consider the valutas separately in their respective monetary systems. Sometimes, however, there is a lytric policy of States which sets up such a parity as its goal, and there is an administrative action for realising it. We call this *exodromic;* it is something different from the valuta policy of the two States within their own borders; it is something new; it is intermittent, and it can be without any effect on the domestic valuta policy of the States. State exodromic intervention is only found in States which have attained a high degree of insight and have the power to give effect to it. The following well-known measures are for the first time brought under a common principle.

The inter-valutary exchange between two given countries is fixed at first without exodromic intervention on the part of the State by the free play of supply and demand on the Bourse, which is the proper arena for this trial of strength.

The State which has resolved on intervention goes down into the arena and brings its forces into play, trying artificially to alter the relations of supply and demand, and going on till its goal is reached. Note then that exodromic control acts with the ways and means of the Bourse, and in this respect the exodromic administration has a certain resemblance to the hylodromic, where there is one in existence. In the case of hylodromy the State wishes to give a certain metal a fixed price within the country, for the State's customers, though not for the State itself. This end is attained by the State playing the part of a giant dealer in that metal; it takes it at a fixed price (Hylolepsism) and sells it at a fixed price (Hylophantism), both in unlimited quantities. So long as the State can carry this through, the efforts of the other dealers in that metal are unavailing and the· price remains fixed. The State, however, must be superior to all the other dealers. It is only by overpowering strength that it settles the bullion price within the country.

The case is similar with the exodromic control. The State must be powerful enough to hold all other dealers on the Bourse in check. Sometimes it has to support the weak supply, sometimes the weak demand, and it must carry all before it if it is to be able to keep the inter-valutary exchange at the parity fixed upon. It is a question of economic strength.

On the other hand, the exodromic control differs very considerably from the hylodromic, for their objects are quite different. Hylodromy aims at settling the price of bullion, and settling it in the valuta money of the home country. In exodromy it is not the bullion price which is to be fixed, but the price on the Bourse of foreign valuta money, expressed in the valuta money of our own country. Hylodromy deals with the bullion trade, exodromy with the foreign exchanges. The objects the price of which is to be fixed are entirely different, it is only the methods that are similar; the State, in both cases, deliberately intervenes to fix the price by its superior strength.

In order to explain exodromic measure—when such exist—we distinguish two chief cases. First let us assume that the currency of both States is hylogenic, and that the hylic metal is the same on both sides, whether gold or silver. If both States have the same hylolepsy, and if, as we assume, for the sake of simplicity, the valuta money is orthotypic in both countries, there is a Mint par between them, and this parity is regarded rightly or wrongly as the natural par between the two currencies.

In this view then the parity between England and Germany comes about, if on the Bourse the pound sterling is worth exactly as many marks as correspond to the gold contents of a new sovereign or a new twenty-mark piece.

The opinion prevails that when two States have the same kind of hylolepsy the inter-valutary parity when it disappears re-establishes itself automatically. Is this view justified?

Observe that the parity can disappear, there can be a German-English exchange which is below par on one side or the other. This fact is known to all who read the foreign exchange column of the newspapers, but is among the things which an auto-metallistic view of currency leaves inexplicable. For the Chartal theory of money and the pantopolic view of exchange this divergence from parity is easily understood.

Granted that there is such a divergence, that the

pound sterling is quoted on the Berlin Bourse not at 20·43, but at, let us say, 20·50 marks. It is then more profitable to send German gold coin to England to be turned into sovereigns according to the Mint standard. German gold coins are accordingly sent till the large payments have been made which by their imminence have occasioned such a demand for English currency. The high exchange of the pound sterling in Berlin will then quickly vanish.

If, conversely, the pound sterling had been quoted far under par on the Berlin Bourse, the English, instead of buying dear German exchange on the Bourse, are far more likely to send to Germany their own gold coins, as these are transformable into twenty-mark pieces; and the low quotation of the pound sterling in Berlin would quickly disappear.

So, it is thought, parity would automatically restore itself, because in case of emergency people could always, by sending their own money, obtain foreign money in order to make specially large payments due abroad.

Here we will not discuss the quantity theory, if interpreted in the sense that the money in one country is diminished and increased in the other, and that this re-establishes the parity. Such an idea is vulgar ignorance.

This " automatic " regulation of the exchange is very instructive. There cannot be any question

here of exodromic administration, for what happens
of itself needs no special provision. Change to
the same metal is often recommended in the case
of metallodromic standards on the ground that the
automatic regulation of the valuta exchange will
immediately follow.

It is, however, extremely doubtful whether the
automaton always acts. The foregoing seems a
correct description of how the exchange rights itself
only when the fluctuations are short and insignificant as no doubt they usually are. The elements of
international indebtedness are numerous and complex whence the total effect of them, as expressed
in the valuta exchange, is not subject to sudden
alterations as far as the first steps are concerned.
Political feeling is only secondary in its effects, but,
when it occurs, it is the Bourses that are affected
by it. In times of peace all this counts for little,
and the valuta exchange seems to be liable only to
slight fluctuations, which may be automatically
overcome. Let us, however, suppose the case, which
cannot be excluded from a general review, that the
balance of payments is permanently altered, *e.g.*
because the one country disposes of its holding
of securities belonging to the other country, or
because the one country ceases to import certain
manufactures of the other country, having found
another source of supply. This destroys the automatic regulation of the valuta exchange.

The counterbalancing export of home currency to the foreign currency would then become chronic. The stocks of exportable money would then run low. If there is a highly developed system of banking, this circumstance makes itself felt through the conversion of bank-notes, that is, through a progressive diminution of the cash reserves of the bank. The bank very soon sees its danger, and attempts all sorts of measures avowedly to preserve its cash reserves. As a matter of fact, it does protect its reserves from exhaustion, but the underlying reason for these measures is something quite different. It is an instance of exodromic administration; measures are taken with the express intention of putting an end to the permanent divergence of the valuta exchange from par. Such intervention, however, shows that the automatic regulation is not always operative.

The intervention is necessary even if, as in the case we supposed, both countries had the same hylolepsy, as, for example, England and Germany. What then are these exodromic measures? They are very various. The best known is the step taken by the bank when it makes the discounting of bills and loans on securities more difficult by raising its rates. Thus fewer bank-notes are issued, and fewer bank-notes therefore will be presented to be cashed. At the same time foreign speculators will be moved to send their capital in order to profit by the higher rates of interest. In this way conscious intervention can cause a situation which creates a demand for German currency in England, when it was Germany whose exchange on England was below par. The low state of the exchange arose, however, from the fact that German currency was not wanted in England. By the intervention of the German Bank the demand which had been absent is artificially created—that is by exodromic intervention, and the exchange is very likely again at par, made so not automatically but by conscious intervention.

This intervention cannot be effected without sacrifice. Those business men who discount bills or take up loans from the bank bear the loss, which consists in a reduction of their profits. If in this way the valuta exchange is again successfully brought up to par, this is not in the least automatic, but is due to intervention by the bank, which alters the conditions of business for its customers, and creates a demand for German money in England. The last point seems to us the most important. The protection of the bank's reserves is only an incident; it is an epiphenomenon which is strongly emphasised by the bank directors. The real purpose of the bank is to bring the German-English exchange to parity. At the same time the re-establishment of the exchange parity removes the causes threatening the reserves. An example from France will make this clearer. In France the bank often protects its reserves without re-establishing the lost parity, nay, without even intending to do so. Therefore the protection of the reserves, important as a part of banking, is not the main point for our purpose. It is not through it that the lost parity is restored. It is therefore not in itself an exodromic measure. But the raising of the discount rate for bills and the raising of the interest rate for loans are exodromic measures, having the welcome secondary effect of protecting the reserves, but by no means themselves mere banking regulations.

Let us now suppose that the two States whose intervalutary exchange is to be regulated have different standards, for example, England with its gold standard and Austria without one till 1892. Such States could set up an exodromic control to keep up a par in view of a reformation of the currency, though in this case there could be no thought of automatic regulation, and there need be no raising of discount and loan rates. Take three examples.

I. The Austro-Hungarian Bank in Vienna resolved to keep the London exchange at the parity which has been aimed at ever since 1892, that is, £10 sterling to 119 gulden. But from pantopolic reasons the exchange fluctuated and had a marked tendency to move against Austria (to 120, 121, 122 gulden). An automatic adjustment was not possible, as in Austria the gold was not valuta; the notes of the State and the bank were so (1892). The following was the method chosen, of which we have intentionally amplified the steps a little.

The bank since 1894 employed a part of its funds in buying a large store of bills on London, and filling up the gap when they matured. As the bank was not acting for profit but for an exodromic purpose, it bought the bills at any price, sometimes at a profit (if on occasion the exchange should be favourable, say 118 gulden to the £10 sterling), but more often at a loss. It was prepared to sell these bills at par, 119 gulden to the £10 sterling, as soon as the exchange moved against Austria. Clearly the bank loses on this transaction, unless its reserve of bills, as rarely happens, dates back to more favourable times. The bank, as a business establishment working for profit, could not have taken such measures, for it was breaking every rule of business. It was acting, however, as an exodromic authority, fulfilling an administrative function, with a view to counteract the unfavourable state of the exchanges. If that reserve of bills was large, business people who wanted to buy English exchange got a sufficient supply from the bank at par. Under such circumstances the exchange naturally fell from 120 to 119, the price at which the bank sells bills on England, and the goal was thus reached; the exchange was at par. The bank's action was an intentional counter-speculation for the restoration of parity, obtained, as it always is, pantopolically. The only difference from normal conditions is that the pantopolic conditions were not left to the blind play of anarchical individual interests, but were arranged by an organising hand, ready and able deliberately to alter them. Such intervention naturally demands sacrifice, which in this instance is borne by the bank. How the bank consoles itself for the loss is its own affair.

It is quite conceivable that unfavourable rates for bills might be successfully countered by this method for long periods of time; only if general pantopolic conditions improve apart from the bank's intervention has the bank any hope of recouping its losses. This happens when, say, English bills are to be had for 118 gulden. Then the bank buys cheap and waits till it can sell at a higher rate. The bank has, however, no means at its disposal to bring about this favourable turn of affairs, so long as it confines itself to the method we have described. Perhaps the State, which has the exchange parity greatly at heart, will be ready to support the bank. In that case the State would take the losses on itself, either partly or wholly. It might issue a loan, and the re-establishment of parity would have been effected at the cost of the tax-payer, who would pay the interest.

II. Under the method usual in Germany, when parity is restored by raising the rates for bills and loans, the burden is passed on to the customers of the bank engaged in such business. There must always be someone to bear the burden. There is no currency system of two countries which in itself and without exodromic administration guarantees exchange parity.

III. A third exodromic intervention was carried out in the years 1892–94 by the Russian Finance Minister in order to stabilise the rouble exchange in Berlin.[1] The object was that the rouble in Berlin should keep the par of 2·16 marks. For this purpose the Russian State put a large amount of German and Russian money at the disposal of a well-known banking firm in Berlin, with the instruction that (1) as soon as the rouble fell below 2·16 marks in Berlin, the bank was to buy all roubles offered to it, at 2·16; (2) as soon as the rouble rose above 2·16 marks in Berlin, the bank was to sell roubles at 2·16 marks. If the stock of both forms of currency at the disposal of the bank were sufficiently large—as it was—this deliberate intervention would keep down all the fluctuations which might have been produced by the other pantopolic conditions. In this instance also the origin of the exchange has not ceased to be pantopolic; but deliberate and powerful influences are added to the other pantopolic conditions. It is evident that here too the maintenance of the exchange entails loss. The Russian State had to hand over a large amount of German and Russian money without any prospect of getting interest on it. Perhaps it could only manage this by means of loans on which it had

[1] See Ph. Kalkmann, *Untersuchungen über das Geldwesen der Schweiz*, St. Gallen, 1900, p. 89.

to pay interest.   Thus the burden fell on the Russian tax-payer.   There would be a sacrifice even if the fluctuations of the rouble in Berlin had been alternately up and down and had lasted only a short time in each case.

It seems, however, that as a rule the Russian exchange insisted on staying lower than 2·16 marks for the rouble, so the store of German money held by the bank became steadily less; and if the measure was to be continued the store had to be replenished from time to time.   Thus the capital for this purpose not only had to be kept in Berlin bearing no interest, but it had to be supplemented.

The Russian Exchequer bore the loss and kept the exchange at par, no doubt for good reasons of its own.   To reduce the loss there is only one way : Germany must be persuaded to increase her demand for Russian currency, perhaps by importing more Russian goods; or Russia must be induced to need less German currency, perhaps by the extension of her own industry.   So long as pantopolic conditions unconnected with the Russian Treasury did not alter, it is questionable whether the exodromic intervention could be successful in the long run.   Do not say that everything was well as soon as Russia had made her new gold rouble valuta, that is, cashed her notes in the new gold coinage.   Perhaps this made the valuta exchange easier to regulate, but this only shifts the question.   Russia can only retain the dromic gold standard once introduced if the pantopolic conditions, which do not depend on the Treasury, so fall out that the desired parity comes about without exodromic intervention. If this is not so, even the maintenance of the dromic gold standard depends on a sacrifice, and the maintenance of the parity on increasing indebtedness. It is a cheap advice, therefore, that the Russian State should go on to a dromic gold standard in order the more easily to maintain its valuta exchange parity. Its problem is the converse. Without the help of the Exchequer, which is very uncertain, the Russian State can only get a dromic gold standard linked with an exchange parity of 1 rouble to 2·16 marks, if the pantopolic relations of both countries allow it, and that depends on the whole economic development.

Where there is no exodromic control, the valuta exchange between two countries depends on the pantopolic conditions of the moment, which work, so to speak, anarchically. This does not mean that the exchange is independent of determining powers, but that the administrations on both sides simply let the valuta exchange go as it likes, without setting up any fixed aim, or making any sacrifices to maintain it.

We find an instance of this in the exchange between Austria and Russia, when both these States were suffering from a régime of inconvertible paper money. Then neither State had the power (and therefore not the will) to set up a parity for the Austro-Russian exchange and to maintain it. It is plain that here there was no par fixed by the nature of things between them. The remembrance of the Austrian silver gulden and the Russian silver rouble does not help towards a parity, for neither State is prepared to restore the old currency conditions. At the most it is felt there was a par in the past that might well be restored, but these are sentimental recollections signifying nothing. The question is whether the State authorities set one up and carried it through administratively, and this was not the case. There was therefore no par, and there was also no exodromic control.

If we look back, we see that the so-called automatic regulation of the exchange is only possible when both countries involved have the same metallodromic system of currency; and even in this instance it is only short and insignificant fluctuations up and down that can be so prevented. In all other cases extensive exodromic regulations are necessary. These measures are always begun by that State whose money is below par, and it can only carry them out at a certain cost. The most important measures are: (1) the raising of the discount and loan rates; (2) the provision of foreign currency through a bank which sells it at par; or (3) finally, provision of foreign currency by the State itself ordering sales at par. In the first instance the loss is borne by those people who are interested in low rates for discount and loans; in the second the burden is passed on to the bank; in the third it is borne by the State.

All these measures, though they may be effectual even against considerable and long-continued depression of the exchange, are limited in their efficacy, inasmuch as they involve loss and require resources able to bear it.

In the last resort the fate of the exchanges lies at the mercy of pantopolic conditions. The State whose currency is below par is only saved in the long run by strengthening its commercial position in relation to the other State, and not by merely altering its currency system, for it is a question of strength, whether a better currency system can be maintained or not. There are both good and bad swords, but a weak man is not helped by being recommended to get a better sword, if his arm is too weak to wield it.

§ 14b. *Synchartism*

From the idea and methods of exodromic control it results that the aim is simply the permanent stabilisation of a chosen inter-valutary exchange parity between two countries. This aim is more easily realised if the two countries have a similar hylodromy, but this similarity is not necessary and it is not enough.

There still remains an arrangement which has been often attempted. We will call it synchartism. When set up between two countries it promises to bring about a stable inter-valutary exchange between them. There is to be a common use of certain kinds of money, brought about by the "monetary unions." The best-known examples are the Austro-German Monetary Union and the so-called Latin Union between France and some of her neighbours (Switzerland and Belgium).

In the Austro-German Union of 1857 the thaler piece was declared to be *synchartal*, *i. e.* this coin was to be used in each of the allied States as obligatory definitive money. In the Latin Union two kinds of money were treated synchartally, the silver five-franc piece and the gold ten- and twenty-franc pieces. These are obligatory definitive money in each of the States of the Union.

Under this system the *synchartal* pieces bear the stamp of the State which issues them, but each State treats the synchartal money issued by the other as if it were its own. Nothing simplifies travelling so much, and the arrangement therefore enjoys a high degree of popularity. But does synchartism in itself create a stable inter-valutary exchange between the States of the Union? Notoriously not. In Switzerland, though synchartal money may be sent in either direction, the French franc is often above the parity which it would seem natural to take for granted. It is in actual fact then not correct to say that synchartism always stabilises the exchange, though in many cases it makes the stabilisation easier.

In the Austro-German Union the synchartism of
the thaler stabilised the exchange at most during
the months November and December in 1858.   From
that time to the dissolution of the Union in 1867 it
did not have the slightest influence in that direction,
nor was such to be expected.   The whole arrangement
springs from ignorance and leads to error.   For
synchartism contents itself with the triumphant result
that the synchartal pieces are " accepted " in all the
States of the Union; they are ranked among the
State's currency.   They are in any case taken at
the State pay-offices, and are often made compulsory
for anepicentric payments.

But their exact position in the currency is not laid
down.   Is the synchartal piece accessory or valuta ?
The conventions are silent on this point, the experts
not knowing the distinction.   But this is, however,
the important point.   If the synchartal piece remains
in the modest accessory position in one of the States
of the Union, synchartism can have no effect on the
inter-valutary exchange.   In Austria the thalers
remained accessory, the bank-notes and State notes
were valuta, and their exchange on Germany underwent violent fluctuations.

In Switzerland at times the notes of the various
banks were only cashed in silver five-franc pieces, so
that this silver coin is valuta ; while often at the same
time perhaps in Paris the notes of the French bank
were cashed in gold pieces, so that there the gold

pieces were valuta. The synchartal nature of the two kinds of money could not stabilise the inter-valutary exchange.

In the synchartal conventions the most important point is left out. It is left undecided whether the synchartal pieces are accessory or valuta. There would appear to be an easy remedy for this. A clause should be added to all conventions that the synchartal money—if there was only one kind—should be treated as valuta by all the States of the Union. If, however, there was more than one kind, it should be laid down in the conventions that a common choice should be made of the one to be treated as valuta. Thus synchartism would facilitate the stabilisation of the inter-valutary exchange. But in actual fact suppose this had been so arranged in the Austro-German Union. Austria would certainly have signed, indeed she did give written expression to her good intentions at the time; but this ingenious paragraph would not have had the slightest effect, because the choice of the thaler or the silver gulden as valuta was an achievement to which Austria felt herself unequal, in spite of a hundred paragraphs in the convention. No currency union can force a State under all circumstances to keep this or that kind of money as valuta, if it entails loss.

It is not unions of States, but valutary federations of States that are needed, and how much chance there is of this the reader can see for himself. Therefore synchartism is extraordinarily unimportant for the stabilisation of the inter-valutary exchanges.

It has, on the contrary, produced a new phenomenon, the synchartal agio, in contradistinction to the internal agio based on the bullion trade and the foreign agio of the *idiochartal* (not synchartal) money, which we have had in mind hitherto.

As we have seen, the internal agio is only possible for accessory money, and, if the State is thought of as quite independent and unattached, the internal agio is only a consequence of the bullion price. If, however, the State is allied with other States through its synchartal money, the position is more complicated, but, provided we have a convenient terminology, quite comprehensible.

The accessory money, which is also synchartal—in Austria the thaler, in Italy the gold twenty-lire piece—may get an agio in two ways: (i) from the price of its metallic pieces; (ii) from its being a means of payment in another State of the Union.

Here then an agio can come about at first in the way we have described, depending entirely on the bullion market. On the other hand, agio—a price higher than the validity of the piece—can arise because the inter-valutary exchange allows it. This is plainly seen in the case of Austria. After 1859 the silver gulden, which had become accessory, had a platic agio (agio of its pieces) to be explained entirely by the conditions of the silver market; for the silver gulden did not come into the synchartal system. The thaler, on the other hand, had also at first an agio as a silver piece. It now acquired another agio, because it was valuta money in Germany and could be used there as a means of payment. This second agio arose from the inter-valutary exchange; the price of German money on the Austrian Bourse had become higher in 1859 than it had been at the end of 1858. There were, therefore, two reasons for the agio of the thaler in Austria. The weaker reason had no effect, for the holder will always choose the greater of two possible profits. From this it appears that there is a third kind of agio. If the accessory money of one State is synchartal with reference to the other, it can acquire an agio, if the inter-valutary exchange of the foreign allied State stands high. This is the synchartal agio.

The agio of the twenty-lire piece in Italy has always arisen in this way, though the double possibility is not so evident as in the agio of the thaler in Austria. This best explains the strange fact that the Austrian silver gulden, which was idiochartal, had a different and smaller agio than the thaler, which was only $1\frac{1}{2}$ times the gulden with the same specific content. It is, however, impossible to explain it without the notion of synchartism and the notions of accessory and valuta money. The metallistic view of money leaves us helpless before such a phenomenon.

§ 15a.   *The Stable Exchange as the Ultimate Goal*

Let us go back to those exodromic measures which seemed at first only a defence of the specie reserves of the central bank, as in 1905 between England and Germany.   For such countries the small fluctuations of the inter-valutary exchange level each other out. It is only in disturbances of some duration that special exodromic measures are necessary, and they are put in action by that State which feels the reserves of its central bank threatened.   They appear to a certain extent as hylic measures or, more accurately, as measures which are meant to preserve the hylo-phantism of the threatened State.   This end is usually the only one noticed, and the fact is completely overlooked that the measures are a roundabout way of regulating the inter-valutary exchange, and are accordingly exodromic.   If all the States of our civilised group had the same hylodromy for their valuta money, exodromic measures would always seem to be in defence of the reserves.   So would it be if the gold standard were universal, and no less if the silver standard were so, not because of the qualities of those metals, but because of the similarity of the hylodromy.   When this book was first written (1905) there was every expectation of the extension of the gold standard to all the most important civilised States.   This measure is really desired because it facilitates exodromic control; and it is only, so to speak, a historical accident that the facility is given by the choice of gold rather than silver as the hylic metal.

The universality of the gold standard has therefore in the last resort an exodromic reason. Once this hylic metal was adopted by the States which were commercially most powerful (in 1871), the less powerful had to join in. If, however, the same powerful States had adopted a silver standard, exodromic reasons would have spoken just as emphatically for the general introduction of the silver standard.

The lively propaganda for bimetallism is really exodromic, at any rate for those who have grasped the chartality of money. Of course the stiff-necked metallists think that it is a law of nature that there should be chrysogenic and argyrogenic money—and none other, that is, no autogenic money. This is childish; but there are better-informed bimetallists who think somewhat as follows : Granted there are a number of States with a gold standard and also a number of States with a silver standard. Between them there is bimetallic France, which for obstructional reasons is sometimes on the side of the silver, sometimes on that of the gold States, and its action serves each time to strengthen the group which is pantopolically at a disadvantage. As long as France remains sufficiently powerful, this system helps to support the inter-valutary exchange of the gold countries with the silver countries, and at the parity laid down in the hylogenic norm for both metals in the law of 1803. Anyone who holds this view is recommending bimetallism for exodromic reasons.

Other bimetallists want to introduce this monetary system into all civilised States. As, however, they have no idea of valuta and accessory money, they give no clear picture of the inter-valutary exchange relations which would then prevail. So much, however, is certain. They expect stable inter-valutary exchanges, or who would benefit ? The metals themselves have no feelings in the matter, and the owners of gold and silver mines ought not to have the chief voice. So even bimetallists of the straitest sect are really led by exodromic considerations. On what grounds have recent currency changes been introduced ?

Changes which were produced by necessity are not considered here. England in the Napoleonic time, France during the war of 1870–71, Austria from 1859 onwards, made autogenic money valuta, because from fiscal weakness they could not do otherwise.

But why about 1860 did France go over to the gold standard, and why did she not go over to the silver standard in 1876 ? Both measures might seem on each occasion to have been pointed out ⸃ by the occurrence of " obstruction." [1] The suggestion, however, was obeyed in 1860 and not in 1876. It is not,

[1] Crowded strongholds. See ch. II. § 10 above, p. 177.

therefore, obstruction which is decisive, but something else, and this could only be the aim of stabilising inter-valutary exchange with the important neighbouring countries, England and Germany. The reason, therefore, was exodromic.

The change to the gold standard by Germany begun in 1871 had for its reason only the unconscious imitation of England, a Power then held to be an economic model. It was only retrospectively through Bamberger's influence that the deeper reason came to light, the stabilising of the valutary exchange in England. The reason was therefore exodromic. Why did not Austria return to the silver standard in 1879, when " obstruction " seemed to point to it ? And why did it in 1892 make laws which plainly aimed at a gold standard ? All the alleged reasons were either illusory or entirely subordinate to one motive, the stabilisation of the inter-valutary exchange with the neighbouring gold States. Here, too, exodromic considerations were decisive.

England's reasons for going over to the gold standard have never been fully explained. I, however, hold it as perfectly certain that England's action was not due to exodromic reasons, for in the eighteenth century, when its pre-eminence in commerce and capital was undisputed, it would only have had to lift a finger to adapt its currency to that of any of its neighbours. England certainly never did that, but always refused on principle. The strong man stands his ground and

the weak man shifts it. England, once possessed of
a gold standard, is the model Power because she is the
strongest. It was because the other Powers wished
to enter into stable inter-valutary relations with her
that, on exodromic grounds, the gold standard spread;
it was the easiest method of reaching the exodromic
aim.

The valuta exchange is therefore the guiding
principle for the choice of a standard, so long as there
is no question of compulsion. Yet it is not every
inter-valutary exchange settlement that is desired,
but only settlement with the Power predominant in
commerce and capital. By exodromic policy we
mean specially the stabilisation of the exchange with
the predominant foreign Power.

England has no such policy, as she is herself the
dominant Power. But all Austria's innovations are
only to be interpreted through her leaning on the
Western dominant Powers.

The enormous extension of the gold standard since
1871 is merely an exodromic approach first to England,
then to the Western Powers in general.

If England in 1871 had had a silver standard, there
would have been the same leaning of neighbouring
States upon her, and this would have meant a universal
extension of the silver standard—if we may be allowed
the exaggeration. If a State with a silver standard
had had the undoubted predominance of England
in 1871, this State would have driven even England

to follow her example, for this State would then have been the leader. It was not the gold standard *per se* that spread after 1871, but the English monetary system, which was the gold standard merely as it were by accident.

"In that case gold *per se* would be quite unimportant in the choosing of a standard? Was it only a question of historical circumstances, which (1871) were then favourable to gold?" If the metallist puts this question, the chartalist can only answer Yes. All middle-sized and weaker States from exodromic considerations either have gone over to the gold standard or wish to do so. England is deaf to all suggestions of currency alteration, for she does not need to trouble herself with exodromic measures. It is the same with the system of military service. If the most victorious State has universal compulsory military service, its neighbours must have it too in so far as they share the same battle-ground. England stands out of it because she does not join in the continental battles. If, however, European States want to enter on a world-wide policy, (*Weltpolitik*), they must imitate England's navy; and, if England chooses to build ships of iron, her rivals must also choose the 'iron standard' in shipbuilding.

§ 15*b*. *Specie Money for Use Abroad, Notal Money for Use at Home*

Another universal phenomenon always goes hand in hand with the extension of the gold standard. Our currencies become increasingly *polymorphic,* and more and more that kind of money which before was considered the only right one falls into the background, though not into disuse.   This is specie money, or, expressed according to our system, *hylogenic orthotypic money,* which in the home country has an increasingly restricted circulation in comparison with notal money.   Here we have in view only those States which keep some sort of specie form for their valuta money.   This is now in most cases the chrysogenic orthotypic form.   In all these cases there has grown up, besides the specie money treated as valuta, a mass of notal money, treated as accessory; and this accessory money is so much in evidence that it would seem almost correct to say that it predominates in the actual circulation.

This state of affairs does not affect the exodromic arrangements, since these only concern valuta money, for which we are assuming the retention of the specie form.

This preponderance of the notal money in the internal circulation is sufficiently remarkable, and needs special explanation.   At first we will give the facts for England, France and Germany.[1]   For

[1] Before the War.—TR.

internal circulation in England payments in sovereigns — valuta specie money — do not predominate. Small sums up to 40 shillings can be paid in subsidiary money, which, as we know, is notal.[1] Smaller sums from £2–£5 are, however, often paid in sovereigns, but preference is given to giro payments, cheques, which are a form of payment, but are not money, still less specie money. For large payments of £5 and over, cheques are often used, but bank-notes are also employed, and these are notal. If in the case of a large payment the creditor desires sovereigns, that is, valuta specie money, he is left to procure this kind of money for himself, in the case of large sums, by cashing the bank-notes he has received. If in England there existed a notal money so broken up that payments of £2–£5 sterling could be made in it (which, prior to 1914, was not the case), sovereigns would be even less used in internal circulation. The receivers of large sums, who afterwards procure sovereigns for them, only do so because they are thinking of their use outside of England.

The case of France is similar. Small sums are paid in small coins. For sums of more than five francs the silver five-franc pieces are used. Both these kinds of money are notal. Valuta specie money, gold pieces, are used for payments up to about fifty francs, that is (before the War), for sums under the smallest bank-note. For larger payments, bank-notes, notal

---

[1] " Notal " is nearly " token." See above, II. § 7, p. 123.—Tr.

money, are chosen, and in this case also it is left to the creditor to cash them (if he will), in valuta gold money, which he as a rule does not do.

The like happens in Germany. Formerly the use of small coins was confined to small sums, now (in 1905) they can be used for amounts up to twenty marks —a great extension of notal payments. For amounts over twenty marks and as high as 100 in the home circulation the most usual means of payment (1905) is gold money, *i. e.* our valuta specie money, but it is often replaced by the cheque. From 100 marks upwards in multiples of 100, payment is usually made in bank-notes, that is once again in notal money; but giro payment is also employed.[1] Even the public pay-offices follow suit in their payments, but do not make giro payments. The cashier who has to pay 1000 marks takes it for granted that the customer wants bank-notes, and asks politely and casually " Do you want gold too ? and about how much ? " Not as if he were refusing to give gold ; but from his experience the customer will be content with notal money, and he only gets out the gold money at the customer's express wish.

All this would be more clearly seen if the fractional notal money were for such amounts that smaller payments could be made in them. In Germany there are small State notes [2] of twenty and fifty

---

[1] See above, Chap. II. § 8*b*.

[2] *Kassenscheine,* Pay-office Warrants.

marks, but very few—so few, in fact, that the customer who wants them could not in 1905 always get them. It is evidently the legislator's purpose that there should not be notal money for these payments of medium amounts; but all that happens is that people are on occasions rejoiced with a sight of the valuta specie money. It does not happen that valuta specie money is made to play a really important part in the internal circulation. It is almost discarded in favour of the notal money, and to discard it altogether would make scarcely any difference. Valuta money is still specie, but for internal circulation it has in the main been replaced by notal money.

Formerly, however, valuta specie money was meant for internal circulation, say in England, when silver money was valuta, and there was some hesitation about the introduction of the small copper coins, which are the most modest kind of notal money. When the Bank of England was founded, it was a long time before its notes won a place in the circulation.

The transformation is not to be explained, in the manner of the metallists, as a progressive degeneration. Chartalism explains it without difficulty. The Chartal property of all money becomes plainer and plainer, with the necessary consequence that for internal circulation notal money is amply sufficient. Notal money, of course, includes discs of precious

metal, *e. g.* silver small coin, or also, in France and
Germany, silver current coin. The platic use of
silver is here a mere historical survival, and does
not conflict with the notality, as this is known from
its genetic condition. In the case of bank and
State warrants the notality is obvious.

These States hold firmly and rightly to a specie
valuta money, not for the sake of internal circulation,
but because exodromic control is thereby made easier.
Specie money has, therefore, for a long time had
only an exodromic meaning. It is one means out of
many for stabilising the inter-valutary exchange. It
therefore discharges a highly important duty. But
the much-lauded specie currency becomes year by
year less important for internal circulation. Observe
what has happened in Austria since 1892. Enormous
supplies of gold coins were struck, obviously to be
used as valuta specie money. But instead of being
put into circulation by apocentric payments, they
were locked up in the strongholds, and purely notal
money was used for internal circulation—bank-notes,
State notes, silver gulden which had become notal.
There was even a creation of new kinds of notal
money, the silver small change under the laws of
1892, and a new kind of ten-krone note, which was
still notal though irreproachably covered. The old
State notes fell more and more into disuse on account
of their unpopular origin (during the war of 1866);
they were, however, not replaced by valuta specie

money, but by other notal money of unimpeachable origin.

In Austria more than anywhere else notal money is clearly the money chosen for internal circulation. The proceeding is masked by the fact that many kinds of notal money are metal pieces, and that many of these are pieces which date back to the system of 1857. They were then specie money, though they have ceased to be so—a fact which the man in the street does not notice and is not meant to notice. This would be an inexcusable deception— if it mattered in the least whether valuta specie money was used in the internal circulation or not. But in reality it does not matter. The Chartal system does not demand it.

It may be answered that Austria was still (in 1905) in a transition state, that the monetary reform of 1892 would not be complete till the gold krone currency was put into circulation, and that the time could not be far off when the bank-notes, old and new alike would be cashed in gold krone pieces, and that then the gold money would be valuta specie money.

This seemed likely to happen, but only from slavish imitation of Western models. If I were asked my opinion, I should say, " Keep to notal money for internal circulation. Even in the West it is usual, and could be universal. Why should medium payments be made in valuta specie money, while

notal money is used for the smaller payments and
notal money also for the larger?" It might be
objected that we should then be deviating from the
aims of the great reform of 1892. Why such enormous
purchases of gold, why the coinage of so much gold
current money, enough to cash all the existing State
notes at a stroke?

But the deviation had already taken place. The
stocks of gold had scarcely been coined into twenty-
and ten-krone pieces when, instead of putting them
into circulation, Government created new notal
money, realising that it had done too much of a
good thing.

It is not very clear why the old State notes were
put away, only to be replaced by other State notes.
A painful memory clung to the State notes of the
war of 1866; people thought they were responsible
for the deficit at that time, while as a matter of fact
the deficit produced the notes and not the notes the
deficit. The dislike of the notes was therefore due
to a historical over-sensitiveness. Austria's lytric
system would, according to the ruling opinion, be
greatly improved if valuta specie money replaced the
1866 notes; but what is gained, if they are replaced
by other money no less notal? Little indeed, for the
discs of the silver gulden are a very insufficient
material cover. People, however, prefer notal
money in silver discs—from historical prejudice,
because they are a reminder of the departed system

of 1857. All reform legislation is mixed up with historical likes and dislikes—the liking for notal silver money being strengthened by its fiscal utility, for it allowed the Treasury to keep a great part of the new gold money. This was perfectly justified by the facts, but it was a concealed departure from the original purpose of the reform of 1892. It was only the concealment that was blamable, not the policy—for why should not political action base itself on prejudices?—but blame attaches to the theorists who give out these prejudices for tenable reasons.

The retention of the silver gulden as current money was justified, because notal money is sufficient for internal circulation, not because it consisted of silver pieces. The State notes would have done as well. Had there been some hope of a considerable rise of silver prices, the retention of the silver gulden might have been justified on grounds of lytric policy.

To sum up,—for internal circulation notal money is almost everywhere dominant and might safely become predominant.

For foreign trade, on the other hand, the valuta money of the State might usefully have the specie form; the most convenient kind of valuta money has been the chrysogenic orthotypic form which existed in England, Germany, and usually in France, and which was contemplated for Austria. It helps to keep the inter-valutary exchange steady between these European States, and, we might add, the United States of America, serving, as we have said above, exodromic ends.

In admitting that internal circulation does not need specie money, we apparently contradict what we have said above as to the dangers of accessory money. Accessory money with a negative agio can drive out valuta money from the State coffers and produce a piling up [1] of accessory money.

If now the valuta money is specie, which I heartily recommend, then the notal money is all accessory, and even the highest and most important kinds will acquire a negative agio. The fear may arise that they will be collected in the State coffers and drive out specie money, so that the State, with the best will in the world, will after a time be totally unable to make specie payments. How is this danger to be averted? With this possibility in view, can we dare to favour the extended use of notal money in internal circulation? Does it not follow, without more being said, that the State can only continue to make specie payments if it always promotes the use of specie money in internal circulation as well as abroad? How can it pay orthotypically if it only receives paratypic money?

These doubts apply to a system which has no scientific lytric control. All State pay-offices are

---

[1] See above, Chap. II. § 10.

thought of as equally busy receiving and making
payments, this being, in fact, their business. If
there were no other pay-offices, the danger of the
accumulation of accessory money would be serious.
But there may be State pay-offices whose express
business it is to exchange accessory for valuta money
and *vice versa*. We will call these Standard pay-
offices. In Germany it is one of the duties of the
Reichsbank to act as a Standard pay-office. It is
ready to convert all kinds of money into one another.
It gives valuta money for all kinds of accessory
money-notes of the Reichsbank, small Treasury notes,
all sorts of small coin and thalers, and will do the
converse, though not on principle, *i. e.* will accept
valuta money, giving accessory money in exchange
(1905).

The other State pay-offices may do this on occasion,
but also not on principle. They rightly decline it as a
duty, they give thought to the means of payment only
when they have to receive or make payments. They
do not undertake to exchange one kind for another.
A special Standard pay-office, of the kind we already
have, is part of a highly developed lytric administration
and is a *sine quâ non*, if the general use of notal money
is to be carried on without mischief. Let the State
arrange its payments in the following way. The
ordinary State pay-offices pay in accessory money,
but the receiver is guaranteed that he can get valuta
money for it on application to the Standard pay-

U

office. As we assume that valuta money is specie,
e. g. gold, this means that the ordinary pay-offices
do not pay in gold, but in accessory money, which
the creditor can convert into gold at the Standard
pay-office. The State provides the gold money under
all circumstances and at whatever cost to itself. If
it pays out all its reserves, it must raise more by
gold loans, that is, procure gold for itself by paying
interest. The gold reserves of the Standard pay-
office must, of course, be inviolable, *i. e.* they must
not be used for any form of State expenditure but
such as involves conversion.

In order to restrict the use of gold for small payments, it would be a good thing to provide convenient
fractional forms of notal money, *e. g.* in Germany for
twenty marks. This would reduce the use of gold for
payments under 100 marks and would make it easier
for the State to keep the Standard pay-office in gold.
Notal money can, of course, both in the technical and
also in the genetic sense only be created by the State,
for as the State promises unlimited conversion
through its Standard pay-office, it naturally cannot
allow the free manufacture of paratypic money.
In our example the Mints must be closed to the
coinage of silver, not because silver is silver, but
because it is not the hylic metal of the valuta money.

The issue of notes by private banks need not be
excluded, as the bank of issue could be compelled
to cash them in valuta money.

The picture we draw is from life except in a few unimportant details. In Germany at any rate (1905) it has been almost entirely realised. The Reichsbank began to act as Standard pay-office; the other State pay-offices only needed to be told to cease making large payments in gold; their customers, if they wanted gold, could always go to the Reichsbank for it.

The view that our gold money ought to be used for moderate-sized payments in the home country seems to me, though harmless, erroneous. It would not arise if our notal money were issued in convenient fractions. Accordingly, it is no degeneration of the currency if paratypic (*i. e.* notal) money comes so much to the front in internal circulation. It really means an increasing recognition of chartality in our means of payments, and it sets free specie money for exodromic ends, to be kept by the Standard pay-office for the customers who need it.[1] With these special pay-offices there need be no piling up in the strongholds.

The theorist, however, must be allowed to think of remote possibilities. He is not pushing a propaganda, but is laying bare the nature of our circulation in order to find its underlying principles. It is perfectly conceivable that these exodromic aims might be attained through hylodromy without the use of specie money. Let us suppose that there was no

[1] For foreign payments.—TR.

specie money in England or Germany, but only bank-notes expressed in sterling in England and notes of the Reichsbank expressed in marks in Germany. On both sides there are Standard pay-offices, which we will suppose convert the notes into gold, not, however, in specie, but in corresponding amounts of bullion by weight.[1] Anyone offering English notes to the amount of £1869 receives 40 pounds troy of standard gold in bars, and *vice versa*. If anyone in Germany offers 1395 marks in notes he receives a pound of fine gold, and *vice versa*. This would be bullion hylodromy. Undoubtedly it would fulfil the hylodromic purpose no less well than the use of specie, and the exodromic purpose also. So specie would become superfluous even for use abroad. But the hylic property of gold would still be recognised in both States, and that is the chief thing. Gold would then be a highly important commodity, but still a commodity, though not in the same sense as other commodities, for both States would have bound themselves to take it and give it at a fixed price. Gold would be a hylic com-modity, which would not be coined, but would be used in bars, not perhaps in general business, but at the Standard pay-office, where the bars of hylic metal would be bought and sold at fixed prices. Of course this would be a great inconvenience, even a step backwards; but clearly it might

---

[1] As in Ricardo's Ingot Plan, 1819.—Tr.

have the desired effect as regards exodromy, and the example is meant to show that the production of specie money could be altogether done away with while hylodromy was retained.

But can hylodromy also be done away with? It is only important in the circulation—apart from private interests—because it facilitates exodromic ends. It is not so important in itself as the metallists believe. For internal circulation it is quite insignificant. Why should not the prices of all metals, whether precious or not, be settled freely? An organised currency remains then no less possible within the country. If the inter-valutary exchange can be settled without hylodromy, hylodromy will have lost greatly in importance; in fact it can, in theory at least, be dispensed with altogether. Let the public man be at ease; even though this is true in theory, it does not follow that hylodromy should be abolished, but only that a different reason should be given for its existence.

It lies with the Chartal theory to explain all currency phenomena on a uniform principle, especially the undisputed fact of the existence of autogenic money. The notion of money must therefore be so framed that money can be thought to originate apart from hylic metal. The notion is therefore widened; but hylic metal may still be used; it is neither excluded nor required. If, however, it is required, it is not because there could not be money without it, but because it helps us to a specially convenient kind of money. Hylogenic money is specially convenient because, being connected with hylodromy, it simplifies the exodromic administration.

Hylodromy is only a means to a higher end, namely, the realising of exodromic control and stabilising of the inter-valutary exchanges. Theoretically it would be possible to stabilise the inter-valutary exchanges even without hylodromy. It is only necessary that the two States concerned should decide on a parity, *e. g.* England and Germany might agree that— fractions neglected—the pound sterling was to be kept at a par of twenty marks.

When this is done, the lytric administration of England decides always to give one pound sterling for twenty marks and that of Germany twenty marks for one pound sterling. Kindly observe that we are not speaking of handing over sovereigns or of double crowns, but of valuta money, which in our own case might be notal, *e. g.* might consist of inconvertible paper money. We are not proposing this; we only assert that it is conceivable, and that the inter-valutary exchange would be stable, so long as this arrangement was retained.

This would be an exodromic control independent of hylodromy. The gold price would fluctuate as the silver price does now, for we assume that hylodromy of gold would have been given up by both sides. What would stand stable would be the inter-

valutary exchange. Let us call to mind what we
have said already about the exodromic administration
of the Austro-Hungarian Bank. If this bank buys
English bills at any and every price in order to sell
them at a fixed price, hylodromy becomes unimportant,
for the bank does not care whether England has a hylogenic currency or not, but buys bills as claims on English valuta money whatever that may be. So with
the arrangement for stabilising the Russo-German
exchange. The Berlin banking firm pays out Russian
and Germany money at a fixed rate one against the
other, a proceeding in which it is indifferent in principle
whether there is hylodromy in both countries or not.
Both these forms of exodromic control are therefore
in principle independent of hylodromy. If this is
the case in actual fact, the possibility of exodromic
control without hylodromy is proved by experience.
There is, moreover, the further consequence that the
specie form of valuta money which can certainly be
dispensed with for internal circulation can also be
left out for foreign trade without affecting the stability
of the inter-valutary exchange.

Theoretically this result is very important.
Hitherto the specie form of valuta money with its
adjunct hylodromy, had found its chief support in
the fact that it made the inter-valutary exchanges
easier to stabilise; but now they can be stabilised
without either hylodromy or specie money. Specie
money therefore has lost its last support, in theory

at least. Bring the existing Chartal system into connection with the exodromic arrangements, and valuta money need not be hylogenic. Gold and silver would then only be necessary for the arts; and could as easily fall out of the lytric system as lead or tin. It would then only be necessary to work out the autogenic currency system in detail. A first essential would be that only the State could create such money; we should next consider by what rules the State should bind itself as to the amount of money to be created. All this, however, is not very pressing, for the innovation is not under weigh. Remember, however, the theoretical possibility of currency systems which insure stable exchanges without the maintenance of hylogenic arrangements. The theorist must be allowed to draw this last conclusion, to show the whole wide bearing of his theory.

Currency is not bound up with the hylic use of metal, either at home or abroad. All metals might be as common as water or as rare as helium; in both cases it would still be possible to have a convenient currency, for hylogenic money, though highly desirable in practice, is not necessary in theory. Money is a creation of law, and, in the last resort, can continue to exist even without hylic metal, because the unit of value is defined not technically but legally. The law indeed only runs within the boundary of the State which makes and maintains it. But States can make treaties and so do away with boundaries;

and this they must do on the disappearance of
hylogenic money, or there would be no possibility of
a stable inter-valutary exchange.

But let us return to the firm ground of the actual
world. Not everything possible or conceivable is to
be recommended, and theory must point out which
of the possible alternatives is the most expedient.
This is not difficult. It is certainly best to keep
hylogenic money while it lasts. In our group of
civilised States it is best to leave gold its hylic use. It
is in particular far the best course to let valuta money
continue in the specie form, as is now the universal
practice, even though notal accessory money supplies
almost the entire wants of the home country.
Hylodromic arrangements are best retained in their
present form. The reasons for this are practical,
and have nothing to do with the essential nature of
money itself. It is the duty of theory to discover
the only tenable reasons, no less than to destroy the
untenable.

The tenable reason is the belief in the par! The
inter-valutary par rests essentially on a decision of
the authorities, as we have seen in the case of Russia,
which stabilised its rouble at 2·16 marks, and Austria
its krone at 0·85 mark. The choice of the equivalent
could be disputed, as indeed it was in Austria. If the
roundabout way of the hylogenic norm is chosen, as
happened in both States, the States then hold themselves bound to abide by that norm for the sake of

their own currency system and therefore to retain that par. Metallistic prejudices would then favour the policy of retention. People think that the parity follows from the hylogenic norm (whereas the converse is the case and the hylogenic norm follows from the parity chosen). That this norm must not be shaken is the first article of the metallistic creed.

The maintenance of the par, once chosen, is made politically much easier if valuta money is left in the specie form in conjunction with hylodromy. Evidently, however, if we choose our currencies from exodromic reasons, any and every method of stabilising the inter-valutary exchange is permissible, and the method most heartily approved on all sides has the advantage. Political prejudices may come in, if they like. Everybody knows that a permanent stabilisation of the inter-valutary exchange is a help to trade. It follows that both sides are eager to have it. Why is it then that the weaker States are always more anxious for it, and are even ready in many cases to undertake changes of standard in an upward direction (as Russia did) in spite of the loss entailed? This cannot be due to commercial interest, but it may well be due to the financial interest of the State. Those States are the " weaker " which are forced to raise loans in neighbouring States. This consideration counts much in the choice of a currency system.

As long, for example, as Austria or Russia was able to raise State loans at home, the stabilisation of the inter-valutary exchange, let us say, with Germany, seemed only advisable on commercial grounds. If, however, these States are counting on raising German loans, foreign creditors have to be considered. They draw annual interest and want to have the enjoyment of it in their own States. But interest is with few exceptions paid in the valuta money of the debtor State. The creditor is therefore greatly interested in the stability of the inter-valutary exchange, that he may know what the interest is worth in his own currency. In this way the weaker States have a strong motive for trying to stabilise the inter-valutary exchange.

The metallists give an explanation which is both instructive and erroneous. They hold that the debtor State has in every case promised to pay the interest in specie. This is only occasionally true. As a general rule only units of value are promised, without the addition of a clause as to payment of specie. If, however, a debtor State pays not in specie but in paratypic money, the metallists consider it bankrupt. Bankruptcy occurs when a debtor ceases to pay, which is obviously not the case here, for payment is made, not indeed in specie, but in paratypic money. This paratypic money would still prove effective if the creditor were actually living in the debtor State, that is, if he were a member of its economic system. As, however, we assume that the creditor is abroad, he at any rate incurs the risk of great loss and he has the feeling of suffering under an at any rate partial bankruptcy. This is a necessary consequence of the fact that money is a Chartal means of payment, an institution the virtue of which is confined to the State which creates it. Every creditor of a foreign State must recognise this and arrange accordingly. It is not an irremediable evil, and chartality need not be abolished to remove it. Chartality must be retained, but supplemented by exodromic control. This is the path which weaker States should tread in the interest of their credit.

Exodromic arrangements are mostly considered from the point of view of the adoption or the retention of a given metallic currency. This is quite correct if valuta money is already in the specie form or is going to keep it in conjunction with hylodromy. People then speak quite rightly of introducing the gold standard or of protecting it if it already exists, for the standard in question can then be described at once by the name of the hylic metal. If, however, the question is of exodromic arrangements in general, theoretically it is unnecessary to choose the round-about way of hylodromy. The currency which a weaker State chooses in order to stabilise its inter-valutary exchange with a more powerful neighbour must be designated not by the hylic metal, but by the name of the State on which the exchange is to be stabilised. For Austria (in 1892) the situation might have been expressed in more general terms by saying that an exodromic connection with England was aimed at, and that this was effected chiefly by the choice of gold as the hylic metal. The exodromic connection is the chief end and the choice of gold a subordinate means.

The stabilisation of the inter-valutary exchange cannot be effected by the Chartal system alone, but only in conjunction with exodromic control. Both taken together constitute the lytric control in its wider bearings. The metallist attends only to the production of the money. The chartalist is not content with this, but brings up an auxiliary in exodromy. For him the ordering of the currency is a branch of the administration of the State. He demands first a conscious, consistent guidance in place of piecemeal measures, suggested by the heads of Mints and central banks, with good practical instincts but without any grasp of theory. The lytric administration must be delivered from this empiricism; after knowing its own aims it must proceed to clearly conscious action, entrusting the direction of it expressly *de jure* to the office which has *de facto* dealt with these matters in the past.

Above all, an end must be made of the antiquated view that the rule of custom is supreme in this department. Even what is called public opinion is of little importance in such a complicated business. It should not be forgotten that the natural man is born and dies a metallist, and therefore cannot judge

our currency system. Least of all should the State
be guided by the "phenomena" of circulation
instead of guiding them, of which the "obstructional"
condition in France in the time of bimetallism was
an instructive instance. The State must remain
master of its own lytric policy, and it therefore needs
a consistent direction, which can only be given from
a central office.

The great controversy between the metallic theory
and the Chartal theory may be summed up as follows :

The metallist defines the unit of value as a given
quantity of metal. He does not understand the idea
of exodromy.

The chartalist defines the unit of value historically.
It therefore becomes a notion which derives its meaning from a particular pay-community in which it finds
itself. The ordering of the relations between different
pay-communities is the duty of the exodromic
administration.

To superficial observation the year 1871 seems
important because it gave the impetus to a hitherto
unheard-of extension of the gold standard. The
silver standard and bimetallism were then doomed
to destruction. The critical eye of theory sees
something quite different. The year 1871 gave the
death-blow to the metallic theory and revealed the
exodromic essence of modern lytric policy.

The Chartal theory does not dispute the historical
and practical significance of metal; it gives metal

its proper place. It was the bridge to chartality; and it is still an auxiliary of exodromy, though not the only one.

The general preference for the specie form of valuta money is due to the recognition that, to a certain extent, it supports the inter-valutary exchange, because our money can then be used abroad, at any rate platically. So far the metallists are right.

But the metallists fail to explain currency systems that have no metal. The chartalist has no trouble in explaining them; they are the touchstone of his theory.

INDEX OF TECHNICAL TERMS

Nominal, 15 seq.
Norm, 61
Notal, 113, 123, 281, 290
Novatory and restoratory, 194

Obstructional, 194
Orthotypic and paratypic, 66

Pantopolic, 222 seq.
Papyroplatic, 69, 108, 123
Par, 218 seq.
Pay-society, 148, 157
Pensatory, 28, 41
Piling up (*Stauung*), 177
Platic, 56 seq., 124, 252
Poise (*schwebend*), 194
Ponderal, 28
Pragmatic, 73, and Pref.
Proclamatory, 30, 38, 43

Rationing (*Contingentierung*), 192
Real debts, 12, 15; payment, 49; satisfaction, 5, 7, 45, 213

Small change, 99
Specie money, 56, 61 seq., 140
Specific, 58
Stabilising, 251, 274 seq.
Standard, 111, 124, 193 seq.; pay-office, 289
Synchartal, 269 seq.

Validity (*Geltung*), 21 seq., 31
Valuta, 105 seq., 165

Warrants (*Scheine*), 69, 71, 95, 137, 282 seq.

Lightning Source UK Ltd.
Milton Keynes UK
UKHW010624060819
347486UK00002B/558/P